CHRISTIAN WOLFF

AMERICAN

Composers

A list of books in the series appears at the end of this book.

Christian Wolff

Michael Hicks

and

Christian Asplund

UNIVERSITY OF ILLINOIS PRESS

Urbana, Chicago, and Springfield

Manufactured in the
United States of America
c 5 4 3 2 1
♾ This book is printed
on acid-free paper.

Library of Congress Cataloging-in-Publication Data
Hicks, Michael, 1956–
Christian Wolff / Michael Hicks and Christian Asplund.
p. cm. — (American composers)
Includes bibliographical references and index.
ISBN 978-0-252-03706-1 (cloth)
1. Wolff, Christian, 1934–
2. Composers—United States—Biography.
3. Avant garde (Music)—United States—History—
20th century.
I. Asplund, Christian, 1964– II. Title.
ML410.W814H53 2012
780.92—dc23 2012005714

CONTENTS

ACKNOWLEDGMENTS

This book began twice. The first beginning was when Christian Asplund invited Christian Wolff and others to the campus of Brigham Young University in the spring of 2006 for a small symposium in Wolff's honor. Asplund, who had studied, performed, theorized, and taught Wolff's music for decades, wanted to showcase the composer's work and allow students to perform his music with him. Asplund also organized a paper-reading session and a panel discussion, both of which he and Hicks took part in.

The second beginning was when, at the end of the symposium, Hicks made this unusual proposal: Would Asplund be willing to collaborate on a small book about Wolff on the condition that Hicks do all the writing? Hicks wouldn't attempt writing a book on Wolff without Asplund's help in navigating the topic. But he had tried collaborating on prose before and couldn't do it. Asplund agreed, he and Hicks devised a book proposal, the University of Illinois Press accepted it, and the work commenced.

Hicks's unexpected four-year stint as the editor of *American Music* (2007–10) slowed the process yet allowed the authors' ideas to foment. Asplund amassed scores, annotated them, interviewed friends of Wolff, and selected and copied hundreds of primary documents from Wolff's personal archive. Hicks interviewed Wolff and kept up an email dialogue with him on many biographical and musical matters, large and small. The two authors discussed, Hicks drafted, shared drafts with Asplund (and Wolff), revised, and so forth. Here now are the results of a happy collaboration.

A collaboration, once begun, inevitably widens. We must thank the many friends and family of Wolff who provided reminiscences and anecdotes, some in miniature, others at length: Robert Ashley, Kui Dong, Petr Kotik, June K. Lewin, Bunita Marcus, Larry Polansky, James Tatum, Calvert Watkins, Willie Winant, Tamsen Wolff, and Tristram Wolff. Other artists and scholars discussed our ideas, read drafts, and made us feel at home in a community of the learned. (Two of those scholars work down the hall from us: Jeremy Grimshaw and Steven Johnson.) David Bernstein and three anonymous readers considered either our initial proposal to the press or a completed draft; all of them gave good advice. British scholars Stephen Chase, Philip Thomas, Laurence Sanders, and Virginia Anderson helped at various times with facts and encouragement. We also think fondly of discussions with students who have played in Asplund's Group for Experimental Music or have attended various related events in which Wolff or the authors took part. We can't recall all those whose thoughts crossed the paths of ours, sometimes lighting the way through a word or phrase. Our deep apologies for any perceived ingratitude.

The archives of Wesleyan and Northwestern universities provided great Christian Wolff and John Cage material; other university libraries, mostly via interlibrary loans, shared of their troves. Our BYU deans, department chairs, and librarians all lifted burdens and opened doors. At the University of Illinois Press, Judy McCulloh encouraged our initial idea and Laurie Matheson coaxed the book into print. Our wives and children graciously consented to suffer from our occasional neglect of them for this book. Here's hoping they'll have labor's fruits to compensate.

This set of acknowledgments is already tipping out of balance for so short a book. But we must describe the lovely patronage and indulgence of our subject, Christian Wolff. Over five years' time he shared with us more than 160 substantive email exchanges, four long recorded interviews, and many unrecorded conversations. He also opened to us his personal archive, which included hundreds of items, from concert programs to letters to sketchbooks to photographs to recordings. We relied on him to tell us his intentions, his influences, and some dates and other personal facts that were otherwise unlocatable. In some cases, we found documentation in his own papers or elsewhere that corrected or refreshed his own memory. In the end he read and commented on all of the chapter drafts. He seems to have enjoyed the ride, bumps and all. So we hope this book will honor his achievements not only by our own academic judiciousness, but by an engaging style that draws the reader into the music and its maker's outlook.

CHRISTIAN WOLFF

Introduction

"I have noticed something . . . about Christian Wolff's music. All you can do is suddenly listen in the same way that, when you catch cold, all you can do is suddenly sneeze."
—John Cage, *Silence*

OF THE MANY ANALOGIES made to music in our time, that may seem one of the oddest—a respiratory one, made not with contempt but admiration. John Cage is not always easy to read, and his meaning here has the ring of a Zen koan. But admirers of Wolff's music may find in Cage's epigraph, as Marianne Moore said of poetry, a place for the genuine. One often responds instinctively to Wolff's music, its impulsiveness, its teasing gestures, its prickly resistance of logic. It is a music often more halting than flowing. But many of us are drawn to it involuntarily, inexplicably.

That may suggest why, in an academic musical culture obsessed with reasons and explanations, theory and analysis, Wolff's music has attracted less than its share of critical attention.[1] Analysis craves methods and systems to which works may be subjected. Musicology craves consistency in a composers' work, at least enough to bundle pieces into "periods" or "phases." And teaching, of course, craves the things that are most easily taught. All of these cravings find little satisfaction in Wolff's music. If Wolff has a method of composing it is to overturn methods from piece to piece. The constancy is change, often radical change even in the vocabulary of a single work. That is bound to work against the stability on which analysis must build.

The restlessness of his imagination prevents him from settling into a Wolff "style," or clearly recognizable idiom—except that he favors epigrammatic utterances, even blunt statements, though often as gentle as spare. They unfold, he says, in "a rhythm that has to do with being surprised."[2] If most musical rhythm is tied to dance—pulse divided and multiplied—Wolff's grows out of a respect for the delicate, barely predictable rhythms of the central nervous system. His rhythms seem more neural than cardiological, not rooted in pulse but impulse. Performers and listeners must consent to respond to at least some of his music in an almost autonomic way. It is not to be savored by mental comparisons with music of the classical canon. It relies on new ways of behaving musically. But within small gestures one often finds floridity: "grace notes and fermatas, you might say, are the two models for [my] kind of rhythm."[3] Sometimes it seems as though Wolff's music were in a latter-day French style—highly ornamented, but now with the main ideas, the ones ostensibly being ornamented, omitted. Ideally for Wolff, these ornaments will combine in a texture of collective spontaneity, "not so much an expression of the player (or composer) as a way of connecting, making a community . . . sometimes involving internally those fluid and precise, and transparent, lines or projections of connection."[4]

Wolff has explained that he writes according to a fivefold "series of ideas." The first, as we have suggested, is *change*. Wolff wants to make new things, even "strange" things. Next is *teaching*. One must convey new ideas to listeners; the ideas may be abstract or quite concrete—even starkly political, as we will see. Third is *unpredictability*. To embrace the world is always to embrace a certain randomness. And the spontaneity one feels in randomness should inform one's music. Fourth is *freedom*. This seems intrinsic to his other purposes, of course. Yet Wolff must assert its fundamental value as an idea in musical behavior. The fifth idea is *noise*. One should explore (and ultimately challenge) that category of sound. What may seem disordered may simply manifest, when close attention is paid, a more complex form of order. Noticeably absent from Wolff's series of ideas are "beauty" or "craft." Though the latter may inform a work's construction and the former derive from it, Wolff subjugates them both to the larger ideas that propel his music. Or, put differently, essential beauty and craft appear in the ideas themselves.

Wolff spent decades as a professor of classics at Harvard and Dartmouth. The very word "classics," of course, implies a standard of taste that can be verified by traditions, even hierarchies of cultural power. That Wolff should pursue "classics" for a career, then, might seem to some bewildering at best and, at worst, hypocritical. But this perceived dichotomy misses the mark. Remember that the classics—especially Greek, Wolff's specialty—exist in either dead languages or ones that remain remote from American English. While Old World classics may be canonical in some sense, they are also arcane. They require a change of mind to appreciate. In that light, Wolff's friend Frederic Rzewski speculated in 1985 why one would be drawn both to ancient Greek tragedy and to experimental music: "What appeals to me personally is that I find myself in the same situation, basically, that these characters were in: confronted with the as yet not-too-clear possibility of a new civilization."[5]

If Wolff's career as a classicist is unusual among progressive composers, so might be his traditional family life. Married for life and devoted father of four children, Wolff may seem much "squarer" than his music. But Wolff found that children in the home provoked new compositional strategies. Interruptibility, for example, had to be taken into account. Collecting ideas and assembling them like a mosaic became habitual. And the lessons learned from children (especially rhetorical strategies) insinuated themselves into new works. Although scholars seldom discuss the effects of parenting on making art, with Wolff one must acknowledge them.

Encountering Wolff the man, one may notice how much his speech resembles his music. He sometimes holds forth with great animation and erudition then stops, suddenly pensive. At the height of a passionate statement he might halt and look into your eyes as though he had just taken a vow of silence. His music displays the same mixture of eloquence and reticence. A florid passage that implies a developmental continuation may simply cease or peter out as though exhausted. What one is left with seems clipped or perhaps simply allusive. Wolff accepts that the listener will mentally supply a consequent for any antecedent he presents.

What is less typical of the man is the juxtapositional nature of many works. While Wolff tends to speaks in paragraphs, logical and orderly, he tends to compose with fragments. That gives his music a sense both of restlessness and whimsy. Were it not laden with so many pauses, one might call the music peripatetic. But agitation gives way quickly to an underlying calm. Thus his gestures take on the character of tentative but exultant moments.

We feel somewhat daunted to assess the work of a composer still living, writing, playing, and speaking about his work. Given the careers of some contemporary composers—Milton Babbitt and Elliott Carter, for example—Wolff could well continue his path, his "series of ideas," for many years that may yet yield surprises. On the other hand, we have had the good fortune of Wolff's help with this first continuous narrative of his life and work. Although it is only introductory, we hope it will illuminate well a composer who always aspires to illumination through music.

If this book is introductory, it is also revisionist. That you are holding this book in your hands is a partial refutation of his reputation as only a member of the New York School of composers, or, indeed, an adjunct to it. Because he had a separate career and did not need to stake claims in the musical landscape in order to survive, Wolff partially receded into the backbrush of that landscape—despite Cage's attempts to push him forward. In this work we try to offer a fresh map to his pioneering.

1 Orpheus in Tennis Sneakers

LATE AT NIGHT, FEBRUARY 27, 1933, forty-six-year-old Kurt Wolff sat with his fiancée Helen listening to Hermann Göring on the radio ferociously blaming the Communists for the burning of the Reichstag. Kurt burst out: "These are madmen. Pack!"[1] Within three days he and Helen had left Germany. By the end of March they had married in London and moved into a house in the hills above Nice, France, where they rented rooms to other Germans who had fled.

Kurt Wolff had long been restless and on edge. Since the 1910s he had sought out and published progressive European authors, including Kafka and so-called "expressionists"—though Wolff rejected attempts to "force on them a shared identity." "Creative achievement," he later insisted, "is always the work of an individual."[2] Having watched the economic crises of the 1920s and a growing reticence among the German avant garde, Wolff had sold his publishing interests in 1930 (the same year he divorced from Elisabeth Merck, with whom he had two children, Maria and Nikolaus). Now, with "madmen" in full reign, "heaven didn't beckon," Kurt explained, "heaven kicked."[3]

But the path to heaven was a labyrinth. Almost a year to the day after she married Kurt, twenty-seven-year-old Helen gave birth to their first and only child: Christian George Wolff. In 1935 the three moved to a house in the countryside near Florence, where they harbored other refugees, until the revocation of their passport in 1938 drove them back into France. In May 1939 they moved to Paris, where, when war with Germany broke out that fall, Kurt was interned for three weeks by the French government. The following year he was interned again; Helen soon followed, sending six-year-old Christian to a convent school for six months. By summer 1940 the family had reunited in Nice. In the following months they migrated west to Spain and Portugal; then, as part of a massive U.S. liberation of exiles, they boarded the *Serpa Pinto*, a crowded ship to the United States, landing on the New York shore on the sunny morning of March 30, 1941.[4]

They checked into the Hotel Colonial, where they stayed for five months before moving into a cramped apartment at 41 Washington Square—the heart of New York City's Greenwich Village, which now teemed with artistic and intellectual exiles from Europe. In December the United States entered the World War. German exiles became enemy aliens, who had to pool their resources and talents to survive. Wanting to elevate European thought in the U.S. book trade, Kurt negotiated with his old friend Curt von Faber de Faur—then at Harvard—for a loan to start a new book company in February 1942 with a mythic name he had used for an earlier company in Italy: Pantheon.[5] He and Helen created a motto for the company's first prospectus: "Classics that are Modern, Moderns that are Classics." With manuscripts and letters spread throughout the Wolffs' apartment, Pantheon quickly became the American voice of the European literary avant garde, including Stefan George, André Gide, and Albert Camus. In 1943, Pantheon joined forces with the Bollingen Foundation to issue the complete works of Paul Valéry and Carl Jung.

After they had completed Pantheon work in the daytime, the Wolffs' nightly routine included Helen cooking the meals and Kurt and Christian washing the dishes, where the kitchen sink became the main site of conversations between father and son about social and aesthetic issues, with literature being a rosetta stone to both. Kurt spoke to Christian either in German or English depending on context and mood. English worked well enough in mundane conversation, and both parents wanted their son to maintain a U.S. identity. But Kurt kept his native tongue alive in his son, according to Helen, not wanting to speak in a "rudimentary" way to Christian, who in 1942 had begun school at Friends Seminary on Sixteenth Street.[6]

One of the many nonsectarian schools founded by Quakers across the U.S. Northeast, Friends became Christian's school from then through all of his precollege school years. It was an old-fashioned, highly disciplined school with classes from kindergarten through twelfth grade, each with about twenty to twenty-five students, including a growing share of emigrés, many of them Jewish. Each subject had one teacher, sometimes a highly trained expert to whom students could go for knowledge beyond the basic curriculum. Openmindedness was as crucial as scholarly zeal. The school had an intramural basketball team on which Christian played in his high school years, despite his father's objections that such sports were ultimately "unhealthy and dangerous."[7] Still, one measured social status at Friends by how many languages one could speak, Russian novels one had read, French movies one had seen, or art galleries one had visited. Christian enjoyed Flaubert and Tolstoy though favored American classics such as *Tom Sawyer* and *Treasure Island.* But Friends offered no musical training, though students sometimes played at the weekly Quaker assemblies where everyone learned to sing hymns between long stretches of silence and the occasional impromptu speaker.[8]

Kurt Wolff, however, knew the music world well. He was an accomplished cellist. His father had been a music professor and choral conductor in Bonn, with ties to Brahms's and Joachim's circles. (Indeed, as a boy, Kurt had met Brahms at Clara Schumann's funeral.) In New York, Kurt and Helen had notable European musicians for friends, especially Adolph Busch and his more prominent son-in-law, Rudolf Serkin. Hoping to lift the cultural sights of their only child, Kurt and Helen exposed Christian to many artifacts of Western culture—paintings, poems, and, of course, music, which for them meant a repertoire dominated by Bach at one end and Brahms at the other. Although associated with modernism because of the authors whom Kurt had published for decades, his and Helen's personal tastes in music rested firmly in historic styles and idioms.

Christian followed suit. He went to as many classical concerts as he could, especially piano recitals, often arriving at intermission when one could enter without paying. Sometimes he booed the new music he heard. He borrowed books of Beethoven piano sonatas, which he picked through, never really learning them to performance level, but coming to know their themes and textures. He did the same with Bach's *Well-Tempered Clavier.* Since his school taught no music theory, he read a book on the "elements" of music—notation, key signatures, basic harmony, and instrumentation. Until his parents got a piano he had to settle for practicing at school or friends' homes.

Despite its lack of music curriculum, Friends fostered much of his informal training in the art. One of his best friends at the school from the seventh grade on was David Lewin (who would become one of the nation's best-known music theorists). Less than a year older than Christian, Lewin was already a fine pianist who had studied with Eduard Steuermann and had even played Schumann's *Kreisleriana* in a Friends assembly. David and Christian sometimes arrived at the seminary around 7:30 (an hour and a half before classes started) to practice four-hand scores at the piano, some of which they played for friends after school. The repertoire consisted of classical masterworks, mostly Bach and Mozart.[9]

On the whole, the two disliked popular music. Christian responded only tepidly to the few Broadway shows he saw and vigorously resisted *Hit Parade* radio programming. While he and his friends knew nothing of the more adventurous jazz then emerging in some local clubs, they did cherish one U.S. vernacular style then resurging: Dixieland. Most Friday and Saturday nights, Friends high school boys would gather at the Stuyvesant Casino on Second Avenue and Tenth Street (or at Central Plaza, a few blocks away) to hear players like Sidney Bechet, Pee Wee Russell, Mugsy Spanier, and James P. Johnson playing hot jazz from the 1920s. The Stuyvesant was one of a few big, barnlike structures in the area with very "live" acoustics, not to mention beer by the pitcher, table dancing, and no one checking IDs. The atmosphere was raucous—far from the Quaker ideals of quietude—and the boys from Friends found the club intoxicating in every sense. In retrospect, two aspects of the music prefigured Christian's later musical practices: virtuosity and heterophony. The Dixieland that enthralled him and his colleagues was, as he later put it, "strong" chamber music—"high-energy collaborative music-making" by spontaneously inventive and technically skilled players.[10]

In the summer of 1948, Kurt and Helen took the fourteen-year-old Christian to a Tanglewood concert of the Juilliard Quartet playing a program of Berg's Lyric Suite, Schoenberg's Fourth String Quartet, and Webern' s Five Pieces for String Quartet. Later, Christian frequently recalled this one event as life changing: he heard for the first time music that he thought not only movingly strange but free enough that he himself might be able to write it—much different, he thought, from the pseudo-Bachian counterpoint he had attempted unsuccessfully before, with little grasp of its rules and procedures.

At about the same time, a family friend asked Christian if he wanted his cache of back issues of Henry Cowell's *New Music Quarterly*. Christian eagerly accepted. As he pored through the pages, he saw the scores to many "ultra-modern" works, as Cowell called them, especially percussion pieces: John Cage's *Amores*, Edgard Varèse's *Ionisation*, and the *Three Dance Movements* by William Russell (the ending of which featured the shattering of a bottle). The harmonies and timbres in these scores struck him as mysterious, the rhythmic configurations unprecedented. With no recordings of these scores at hand and, so far, no opportunity to hear them in concert, Wolff had to appreciate mostly the sheer image of difference they presented. Nevertheless, he could hear some modernist pieces on WNYC radio, including *Ionisation* and Milhaud's early *Oresteia* setting.[11] In these works he found models of radical attitude, if not of specific technique. Together with what he had heard at Tanglewood and the Stuyvesant Casino, the compositions began to give him vague ideas of music that had the rigor of European masters but the happily cluttered textures of Dixieland.

Attempting to follow the examples he had heard and seen, he wrote a few dissonant miniatures on the piano his parents had now acquired. Sometime in 1948, friends of the Wolffs arranged for Christian to audition them (along with some classical standards) for their neighbor Carl Friedberg, an aged former pupil of Clara Schumann. Although not impressed with Christian's playing, which even the fourteen-year-old knew was lackluster, Friedberg thought Christian's compositions had potential. He encouraged the young man to spend time improvising at the keyboard. Wolff began to do so as a means of generating ideas—leading his mother, a friend recalls, to greet him as he improvised with the simple question, "Komponierst du?"—"are you composing?"[12]

Late in 1949 Christian began piano lessons with Grete Sultan, another German who had come to the United States in 1941. Wolff knew some of Sultan's staunch performances of old-world classics but only gradually came to realize her devotion to new music, especially when he turned pages for her on a set of pieces by Hans Apostel she played at Columbia University. He learned she had even met and played pieces by Henry Cowell, publisher of the *New Music* scores that had beguiled him. With Sultan's guidance he began to practice the op. 11 of Arnold Schoenberg, his first playing of the kind of music he had heard at Tanglewood.

Wolff's lessons with Sultan were a mixed success. On the one hand she tolerated and even encouraged his bringing of small, quirky original pieces to lessons. On the other hand, he practiced less and less, arriving at each lesson unprepared to play but with a new composition or two in hand to show her, brief pieces that imitated Schoenberg and Bartók. After weeks of this, she told him he needed to find someone who could help him with composing; she could not. Christian thought immediately of Varése, who had once knocked on the Wolffs' door and introduced himself, and whose *Ionisation* Christian knew. But Varèse's reputation for severity and for courting excessive devotion from students warded Christian away from the idea. Sultan, meanwhile, thought of a friend of Merce Cunningham, the dancer who lived upstairs from her. Merce's friend was another *New Music* percussion composer, who had been introduced to Sultan by Henry Cowell in 1945: John Cage.

In March 1950 Wolff made an appointment to see Cage at his Lower East Side tenement on Monroe Street, a rundown flat next door to a burned-down rat-infested bakery. With no nameplates on the doors, Wolff knocked on one door after another until he found Cage's on the top floor. He showed Cage a few small, densely dissonant pieces, including two for violin quartet and a song cycle for voice and two violins on a text by a French medieval poet. After seeing these works, Cage agreed to teach the young man. When Christian left, Morton Feldman recalled, Cage "came downstairs and tumbled into my apartment, shaking with excitement. He just couldn't get over the music that was brought to him, especially from someone so young."[13] Cage wrote enthusiastically to his friend Pierre Boulez: "I have a wonderful pupil. He is sixteen and his favorite composer is Webern. He has great intelligence and sensitivity. What's more, he was born in France. His name is Christian Wolff."[14]

At the time, Wolff knew only the Webern of earlier works, especially the op. 5 pieces for string quartet, which Wolff had heard at Tanglewood. But Cage had hand-copied the New York Public Library's score to Webern's Symphony, "since it was nowhere to be bought."[15] Probably relying on what he had learned from Boulez in a visit to France in 1949 and from Leibowitz's newly translated book on the Second Viennese School, Cage had begun an analysis of the row forms in the first movement of the Webern Symphony. He assigned his new student to finish labeling the row forms in that movement, a rigorous indoctrination into twelve-tone pointillism.[16]

For six weeks, one lesson a week, Cage also gave Wolff exercises in species counterpoint (fig. 1) and taught him his method of organizing a whole piece so that all the time spaces, both micro and macro, were in proportional relationships.

The purpose of these technical studies, Cage explained, was to learn how one develops discipline. After the formal lessons stopped, Wolff kept writing music and met with Cage from time to time, the older mentor not only advising Wolff on his work, but introducing him to the music of Erik Satie and Virgil Thomson, from both of whom, Wolff recalls, "I first got a sense of how vernacular strains might be compatible with modernism."[17] Cage, following the example of his former teacher Arnold Schoenberg, didn't charge Wolff.

However adventurous Cage was in his ideas, he was a strict academician, whose notion of music abandoned expressivity and relied on a priori forms not built from up from "content" (e.g., exposition, development, recapitulation) but from proportional schemes—numbers and groupings of measures or beats, into which one could pour short musical gestures, including percussive "noise." And he elaborated these proportional schemes not by intuitive lengthening of segments but through the nesting of proportions, mapping temporal ratios onto various structural levels, from micro to macro. It was an academicist modernism that took its cues from Webern, as Webern had taken his from early sixteenth-century counterpoint.

Figure 1. A page of Wolff's first species counterpoint exercises with corrections by John Cage. Wolff Papers. Used by permission.

Cage urged Wolff to compose with only a few notes in scale segments. This began with solo monody, then advanced to pieces for multiple instruments. (Wolff also explains that, "one day, I was browsing through this book about medieval music . . . and I saw a musical example with some close two-part counterpoint with very few notes, and for some reason that image stuck in my mind.")[18] By May 1950 he had completed three songs for voice and flute, four for voice and two percussionists (a grouping derived from Thomson), and four instrumental duos—none of them involving piano.

In June, Wolff wrote a piece for just three adjacent pitches, the Duo for Violins, which became his putative op. 1. It consists entirely of the pitches D5–E♭5–E5 played in different rhythmic and timbral combinations for eighty-five measures (almost four and a half minutes). For the duo, the sixteen-year-old Wolff worked out a rational scheme, one that put a new twist on "twelve-tone" theory. He surmised that a group of three pitches deployed between two solo-line instruments could yield twelve different "sounds." Each individual pitch played alone makes a sound. There are also three dyadic simultaneities (pitches 1 + 2, 2 + 3, and 1 + 3). So far, then, a total of six different sounds. But Wolff adds to that the various skewerings of the dyads-that is, dyads in which the two pitches are not attacked simultaneously or not held the same length of time. So we have:

1 to which 2 is added, then both held to a simultaneous ending

or

1 and 2 simultaneously attacked but held for different lengths

—and so on with the other two dyadic combinations. These skewerings of the dyads, then, create six additional "sounds," giving Wolff a total of twelve different sounds from one three-pitch set for two solo-line instruments.

For his remaining year of high school, Wolff continued developing similar techniques from the Webern-Cage axis: short, lean pieces with only few pitches or fixed "gamuts." For Cage, a "gamut" was simply a collection of sounds, each an individual pitch or noise or clump of either. These gamuts would take the place of scales.[19] Each gamut could be arranged into a single monophonic line, a "melody" of assorted sonorities. Such lines could then be deployed in preconceived groupings of measures or beats—often "square-root" forms, organized into A × A formal structures or time lengths. The "melodies" of gamuts, draped over these symmetrically nested forms, constituted the whole substance of new works.

Thus the pieces in Wolff's early opus—which set the pattern for all his subsequent compositional periods—were epigrammatic, not only for their brevity, but for the terseness of their gestures. Silences also filled the pieces, rendering the musical fabric allusive: the spaces resembled the gaps in short-line American poetry, inviting the listener to focus on individual words or brief phrases. These early pieces (and most that followed) often seemed like little patchworks of musical haiku.

The duo was the first of a series of works with less than the total chromatic. Although defying the hyperchromaticism of the Schoenberg and Webern he loved (not to mention most of Cage's work), Wolff used limited-pitch pieces to refine the discipline Cage had enjoined. These nine works, all completed before Wolff graduated from Friends Seminary in 1951, proved some of his most prescient and influential. While they share a common spirit of constraint, each work broke some new ground for him, suggesting a peripatetic spirit that would energize his work for decades and fuel the more spontaneously changeable (he would say "efficient") semi-improvisatory works for which he would become best known.

Several of the compositions of this period seem like tropes on the technique of Duo for Violins.[20] Consider the String Trio, for example. In the duo, the "melody" consisted of pitches sounding alone, simultaneously, or overlapped in varying ways. In the String Trio, Wolff increased the number of instruments by one and added double stops to the texture. He also splayed the harmony: where the duo had three half-step-related pitches, the trio used three half-step-related pitch *classes* (C♯–D–D♯), fixed in their registral placement but spread quasi-symmetrically over a span of four octaves (C♯2, D3, D♯4, D5, C♯6). Formally, the piece unfolds in a strict ABA for the first twenty-seven measures (marked by a double bar), followed by BAABA, in which each of the "expositional" A and B segments is subtly varied, typically by minimal elongations or compressions of time lengths. It exemplified a trait to which Wolff would recur throughout his career: doggedly formulaic structures tempered ever so slightly by momentary intuitions.

His next piece, the Serenade (for flute, clarinet, and violin), broke new harmonic ground, using three pitches spaced in perfect fifths: E4/B4/F♯5. This overtly diatonic framework, deployed in a *moto perpetuo* pointillistic texture, oddly foreshadowed the classic minimalism of the next generation. Formally, Wolff adapted Cage's "square-root" form as his scaffolding. He starts with this set of proportions 2:1.5:3:2.5:1 (= 10), which represent numbers of measures in $\frac{4}{4}$ (or, in other words, forty beats arranged into groups of 8:6:12:10:4). In Cage's method, one would take that series to represent the number of sounding repetitions of the forty-beat pattern in each section of the piece, thus:

2 × (8:6:12:10:4)
1.5 × "
3 × "
2.5 × "
1 × "

Rather than this essentially additive approach, Wolff took a multiplicative approach, mapping the same *proportions* onto each section. Thus, the twenty-measure first section divides into five segments with the lengths of 4:3:6.5:2 measures each (each segment marked by a dynamic shift). The second section (15 measures) divides into five sections in these proportions: 3 (12 beats):2.25 (9 beats):4.5 (18 beats): 3.75 (15 beats): 1.5 (6 beats) (= 15 measures, or 60 beats). And so forth.

After writing a four-pitch trio (January 1951), Wolff wrote his first work based on the "chart" technique Cage had used in his Concerto for Piano and Orchestra.[21] This technique involved the composer making a box of squares, like a small chessboard, across each row of which he wrote series of sonorities. Wolff took that basic idea but modified it in *For Prepared Piano.* This four movement piece composed in the spring of 1951 used Cage's technique of applying objects to strings to turn the piano into a small pseudo-percussion ensemble. To structure the piece, Wolff made four 5 × 5 squares into which he wrote vertically (up, down, up, down, etc.) sonorities from gamuts he had created for each square (each sonority from one to five pitches in density):

I = 7 sounds
II = 12 sounds (+ 1 that sounded only once)
III = 10 sounds (+ 1 that sounded only once)
IV = 6 sounds (+ 3 that sounded only once apiece)

(Only by the fourth movement had all twelve pitch classes appeared.)

Then, having filled in each box vertically, Wolff wrote out resultant horizontal lines, packing various linear combinations into the twenty-five $\frac{4}{4}$ measures of each movement, with irregular lengths of rests among them, privileging silence to a degree not known in his earlier works. This method, of course, permutated the sounds in a way systematically contrary to their actual composition. Thus, from that process, Wolff arrived in the first movement at his seven sounds arranged in this order:

1 2 3 2 3 4 2 3 4 2 5 3 4 2 6 1 3 7 2 3 5 1 5 4 6 5 3 7 6 1 2 7 7 6 2 4 4 1 4

Their constructive origins notwithstanding, one may sense a pleasingly "organic" unfolding of elements: the gradual introduction of each new sound one at a time (after the initial three have sounded in succession) until no. 7 finally arrives as the eighteenth attack in the piece.

Wolff's willful execution of "non-intentionality" impressed Cage deeply. In *For Prepared Piano,* Cage explained to Boulez at the time, Wolff had created "music in a structure which fixes sounds in a preconceived space without regard for linear continuity."[22] "It was Wolff," Cage later explained, "who [in this piece] made clear to me the necessity to renounce any interest in continuity. It was he who, in order to 'let sounds come into their own,' wrote music vertically on the page though the music was to be played horizontally." Thus Wolff had "*discovered* geometric means for freeing his music of intentional continuity."[23] In a 1959 essay, Henry Cowell famously said that Cage and his New York School colleagues (Wolff, Feldman, and Earle Brown) were "four composers who were getting rid of the glue." That meant, Cage explained, that while other composers "felt the necessity to stick sounds together to make a continuity, we four felt the opposite necessity to get rid of the glue so that sounds would be themselves." Cage then said, "Christian Wolff was the first to do this."

Though impressed by Wolff's ideas, Cage encouraged his student to get practical experience by writing and playing for dancers. Wolff arranged with Jean Erdman—a friend of Merce Cunningham and the wife of Pantheon/Bollingen author Joseph Campbell—to play for a few of her classes and for at least one of her students' dance recitals. At that 27 May 1951 recital, which included works by Morton Feldman and Lou Harrison, Wolff played piano for six of the ten numbers. These included pieces by Schoenberg and Bartok, as well as two of his own, one of which being his first public attempt at improvisation. It was a stop-gap solution for having to play for a dance he had thought wouldn't be ready (and hence hadn't written a piece for), but ended up on the program. To improvise in this circumstance wasn't an aesthetic choice, of course, but a pragmatic one. Wolff recalls it was "not so much 'spontaneity' as being ready as a performer to do what's necessary to keep things going."[24]

The month after that recital, he graduated from Friends Seminary and his parents took him on a trip to Europe. Cage got Christian to spend a week in Paris with Boulez, who showed Wolff around the new music community there and even gave him the manuscript of Boulez's first piano sonata, inscribed "in admiration of his so precocious talent from one who is nearly an old man."[25] Boulez "basically babysat me," Wolff said, recalling that "I spent all my time with him and he introduced me to all his friends and we hung out together and we showed each other music," including some by himself and Feldman.[26] During Wolff's visit, Boulez wrote a letter to Cage affirming that Cage and Boulez were then "at the same stage of research."[27] Boulez did not like Wolff's limited-pitch technique, though, nor did he think highly of his compositions, he wrote to Cage. He urged Wolff to use the complete set of all twelve pitch classes—which Wolff would exuberantly do a few months later.

While this trip introduced Wolff to the world of the European serialists, it also showed him how differently he and his New York colleagues had come to view musical construction. Where Webern had inspired the Europeans with his orderliness, the Americans prized Webern's terseness. Boulez and his compatriots busied their textures with elaborate embellishments of serial schemes. Cage and his friends increasingly pared down their textures, constructing delicate isolated gestures that were like constellations in their sparsity. Inference became the ideal.

After his return to New York, Wolff began a kind of graduation piece—a summation of the techniques of his mentors (Cage via Webern and vice versa) coupled with an expansion of forces. The title, *Nine*, suggests some compositional constraints:

- 9 instruments (flute, clarinet, trumpet, horn, trombone, celesta, piano, two cellos)
- 9 pitches (E2, F♯2, F♯3, G♯3, A4, E5, B5, C6, D7—the pitch classes of an A minor ascending melodic minor scale, with the E and the F♯ doubled)
- a 9 × 9 grid, into which Wolff would place sounds from an enormous gamut[28]

He did the latter by laying out various kinds of continuities in geometric patterns. Each continuity could consist of different relationships. For example: consider an isolated block chord of four pitches, played by four instruments at the same dynamic (this is the "purest," most stable harmonic unit in the piece). One then has many possible "continuities": different pitches (some or all), different instruments (some or all), different dynamics (some or all), overlapping the chord with one or more pitches sounded by another instrument (or other instruments), spreading out the attacks of chord tones, expanding the number of broken-chord tones (to as many as nine), and so forth. Any such variant could be chosen (or combined) in a given square; successive squares in diagonal or other patterns would follow the same kind of "continuity." Having "composed out" the grid in this way, linking one sound to the next along a given line of boxes—and including occasional empty boxes, connoting longer rests—Wolff could then proceed from left to right (as in *For Prepared Piano*) to realign the continuities into discontinuities. He then essentially transcribed the piece from the grid, deploying rests as needed, recasting the meter from 81 measures of $\frac{4}{4}$ into 162 measures of $\frac{2}{4}$, and occasionally changing the meter (e.g., to $\frac{3}{8}$) for ease of reading.

Completed in September 1951, *Nine* became, in effect, Wolff's hybrid of Webern's Symphony—a rigorously organized pointillist piece for mixed orchestral colors—and Cage's Sixteen Dances—a nine-instrument chart-based gamut piece completed in January of that year. Where Webern had used a twelve-tone technique with canons, Wolff used block-by-block non-twelve-tone musical "tiles" in a mosaic of sound. It was atonal and tightly controlled on one hand, but pitch restricted and intuitive on the other. In later years, Feldman would call it the "masterwork" of this period.[29]

By then Wolff had drawn from Cage the fundamental ideas, habits, and relationships that would guide the rest of his compositional career. The ideas included an overall nonexpressive constructivism; the primacy of rhythmic schematics for a piece; the power of silence; the technique of sonic "gamuts"; the breadth of usable continuities from sound to sound; and the value of all kinds of ideas for rethinking music. Species counterpoint gave Wolff a sense of discipline and calculation at a note-to-note level; improvisation freed Wolff for the spontaneity that would pervade his best known pieces. Cage brought Wolff into a nurturing community of likeminded artists (including painters). By Wolff's high school graduation, he was an inseparable member of what would become known as the New York School of composers, consisting of Cage, Feldman, Wolff, and Earle Brown (husband of Carolyn [Rice] Brown, a new dancer in Merce Cunningham's company). And Cage taught Wolff that only performance constituted the completion of a work. Hence, Wolff would soon become less true to "ideal" rules than to do-it-yourself methods that would facilitate performance.

But Cage repeatedly said that "I learned more from [Christian Wolff] than he did from me."[30] That claim may be as much generosity as fact. But Wolff certainly provided three things that notably altered Cage's compositional career. One was the calculated discontinuity of *For Prepared Piano*, the "letting sounds be themselves" with which Cage credited Wolff. Another was Wolff's gift to Cage in return for free lessons. In 1950 Pantheon had published a fine two-volume edition of Cary Baynes's English translation of Richard Wilhelm's German version of the Chinese classic *I Ching*.[31] "Because I was getting free instructions and we were friends," said Wolff, "I would try . . . to make my contribution" to Cage's work. Wolff thought the new *I Ching* edition might interest and even influence Cage, partly because he knew his teacher's interest in Jung, who wrote the preface to this edition. The *I Ching*'s first volume also contained magic squares and, at the end, a fold-out chart of hexagrams that resembled magic square symmetry.[32] So Christian gave the set to his teacher (the first of many Pantheon publications he would give Cage). "I was struck immediately," Cage said, "by the possibility of using the *I Ching* as a means for answering questions that had to do with numbers"—better even than the magic square.[33] The *I Ching* suggested to Cage a mechanism for routinizing chance operations—that method for which Cage is perhaps best known.

But a third, broader and more lasting influence on Cage may actually have come through Christian from his parents. Cage had pursued a European artistic lineage by studying with Schoenberg on the West Coast. But Cage found in the Wolffs an entrée into both the Old and New World intelligentsias, one for which his friendship with the proprietors of Pantheon Books was the best credential.

Kurt and Helen invited Cage to dinners and parties, whose guests included Alan Watts, Joseph Campbell, and other authors published by Pantheon. Already something of a polymath, Cage eagerly embraced this heady company and referred to their works and ideas for decades thereafter. As early as 1954 Cage wrote to Helen Wolff of "my love for you and a sense of responsibility to you and to Mr. Wolff (through my relation to Christian) from which I am not free."[34]

Christian, though, was too young to enter Cage's social circle fully, the older art crowd that lingered in long, nightly discussions at the Cedar Tavern. ("Well, I might tag along," Wolff said, "but when it was suppertime I . . . had to negotiate it at home.")[35] Still, he knew how hard Cage and Feldman struggled as composers to pay the bills. He decided not to attempt, like them, a career as a composer. If Wolff had mimicked Cage in attitudes and methods, he rejected the hand-to-mouth existence that seemed to nourish Cage's monastic approach to craft. And while Wolff's parents exemplified to Christian a stolid self-reliance, their pragmatism tempered any of the speculative adventurousness Cage prized. So in September 1951, Christian enrolled at Harvard, where his bookishness led him into classics, a field suitably esoteric, yet bankable as an academic career. But by then his reputation as a New York School hero was already fixed. Years later, Feldman would characterize the young scholar of Greek and Latin with his own classical metaphor: Wolff, this inventive and prescient composer in their midst, had been "Orpheus in tennis sneakers."[36]

2 Situations of Too Extreme Difficulty: 1951–1959

AFTER MANHATTAN, WOLFF FOUND Boston sleepy and sedate—a perfect place to study the canon of dead languages, but less apt for radical experiments in sound. Harvard itself was notoriously conservative, not only in its social habits and politics but in its cultural life. Music composition on campus was staid, though avid, its thriving academic program overseen by Walter Piston and Randall Thompson, both eminent composers with Old World regard for form, coherence, and balance. Although they guided their students (who included Leonard Bernstein and then neoclassicist Elliott Carter) into the modernism of Stravinsky, Bartok, Hindemith, and even Schoenberg, Piston spurned Cage and his ilk—more puzzled than dismissive, he found the experimentalists amusing but artistically marginal.[1] Understandably, Wolff shied away.

But he continued to compose. From the time he entered Harvard in 1951 until he enlisted in the army in 1959, all but one of Wolff's surviving compositions were piano pieces—seven works in which he moved from Cageian gamuts and prepared piano to utterly new configurations of musical materials and composer-performer relationships, though still generally within Cageian overall forms. To write for piano—Wolff's own instrument—fostered innovation and evolution, since it relieved him of the need to manipulate instrumental timbres: the piano became, in effect, a limited color gamut within which to explore pitch and rhythm.[2] At the same time, he had not only himself as a potential player, but also Cage and, more important, Cage's friend David Tudor, whose superb technical skills, severe discipline, and zeal for the newest and opaquest music had become the New York School's virtuoso ace in the hole.

Tudor began playing Wolff's *For Prepared Piano* in the summer of 1951, at Boulder, Colorado, in his first full recital of New York School works. He became the work's champion for the next six years, playing it throughout the United States and Europe. *For Prepared Piano* was the most immediately appealing of Wolff's teenage works for its delicacy, exoticism, and allusiveness. At Tudor's now legendary Cherry Lane Theatre performance in New York City, January 1, 1952, the piece sat alongside massive works of Boulez, Cage, and Feldman (the three composers who had bonded with Wolff to complete a joint set of essays explaining their respective musical "researches").[3] The *New York Times* reviewer understandably found Wolff's small set—dwarfed by the music that surrounded it on the program—perhaps the most charming on the program: they were "quite attractive. . . . brief and wistful, and lonely in their effect. It was like listening to rain dripping from an eave and splashing and dropping and clanking as it fell on different objects."[4]

In the weeks following that Boulder recital, Wolff wrote a new piece he titled *For Piano I.* It contained only nine pitches (D♯1, E2, F♯2, F♯3, G♯4, G5, C♯6, G♯6, B♭7), thirteen durations, and nine dynamics, all reconfigured in often brutally difficult ways. In one instance, one has to play a chord spanning over four octaves with different attacks, durations, and dynamics: that is—using actual fractional values of durations—a sixth note B♭6 (at ***ff***), a sixth note C♯6 (at ***p***), a fifth note G♯4 (at ***f***), and an eighth note F♯2 (at ***ppp***). What occasioned such nonrecurrent combinations was Wolff's use of a gamut of sixteen different densities, a "density" being defined by the number of pitches sounded anywhere within a given space. For example, the first density consisted of three pitches sounded within a space of nineteen sixteenth notes; the second density, seven pitches within the space of three eighth notes; the third density *no* pitches sounded within the space of seven eighth notes; and so forth. These densities could also be superimposed, allowing the smaller one to occur anywhere within the space of the larger one. The sequence and superimposition of densities, though, were determined by chance procedures.

A year later, Wolff produced that piece's unlikely sequel, *For Piano II,* which used all eighty-eight keys of the piano—Wolff's response to Boulez's critique of his restricted-pitch technique—with tempi flexible (within given limits) and dynamics (except for a few) chosen by the performer. The piece unfolds in four parts that move gradually from intuitive hyperchromatic gestures toward increasing logic and order: The first part has no discernible method, simply the free use of many pitches scattered around the keyboard. Following a brief pause, the second part continues this seemingly haphazard unfolding, bringing in all the remaining pitches. The third part (with no pause preceding it) features five fixed "scales" of thirteen or fourteen pitches apiece and a fixed number of rhythms and rhythmic structures; after another pause, as between movements, the fourth part continues the rigors of the third. Wolff used the top and bottom notes of the keyboard only once each, and others more, often multiple times in close succession, giving fleeting hints of the staticity of his earlier works. Still, the effect is of a ferocious pointillism, wildly traversing the keyboard in ways he had not previously attempted. Dozens of this piece's simultaneities require gymnastic hand deployment (as in the sixth measure, which called for B2, E4, and B♭5 to be played essentially together while one hand holds a long D♯4 that had been attacked amid an even more improbably dispersed set of pitches in the previous measure, including a simultaneous attack of C♯4 and F7).

Tudor learned the piece, drove up to Harvard with Cage and premiered it at the April 1953 Festival of Harvard Composers—where it protruded sharply from an otherwise more conventional program of student works—and kept the piece in his repertoire for the next three years, performing it in recitals that, almost predictably, the *New York Times* dismissed as "hollow, sham, pretentious Greenwich Village exhibitionism."[5]

Meanwhile, Wolff's compositional output slowed in 1954, with only one work, the Suite for Prepared Piano (again, for Tudor), combining the exotic sonorities of *For Prepared Piano* with the more jagged rhetoric of *For Piano II.* During the 1954–55 school year, Wolff focused on completing his honors program in Classics (i.e., Greek and Latin), barely cracking the Harvard music scene but making the occasional foray to New York and a summer trip to Europe though avoiding France, fearing he could, by his birth status, be inducted into the French army.

The year 1955 proved a culmination for Wolff and his family. In the spring of that year Pantheon published Anne Morrow Lindbergh's *A Gift from the Sea.* By the end of the year it had sold more than 600,000 copies in the United States alone, dramatically lifting Kurt and Helen's prestige and bargaining power.[6] Graduating that spring from Harvard with a magna cum laude bachelor's degree, Christian also received Harvard's Richardson Prize, a Woodrow Wilson Fellowship, and a Fulbright scholarship to study language and literature at the University of Florence for the 1955–56 school year. On the boat to Italy that summer, he sketched ideas for a new piano duo and also befriended the young composer Richard

Maxfield, a fellow traveler then on his way from studies with Milton Babbitt to work with twelve-tone composer Luigi Dallapiccola. Whatever Wolff learned of literature in Florence was overshadowed by musical adventures—a trip to Cologne, for example, where he visited the loquacious Karlheinz Stockhausen, who played Wolff three hours of recordings of new European music, mostly his own. (Wolff's reputation had preceded him, though: Tudor had written to Stockhausen, likening Feldman's and Wolff's piano works to Stockhausen's *Klavierstücke* in their "psychic status of great definition," which he considered the authentic "path," whose "more rigorous mastery of material should reveal easily the higher spiritual states."[7]) In Florence, Wolff occasionally played his and Feldman's piano music for small gatherings and discussed with Maxfield what Wolff considered Babbitt's "absurd preoccupation with pitches." He also attempted composing, though after five months had only about two minutes of a trio to show for it.[8] In March 1956 Cage wrote Wolff about a six-week series of concerts he was planning for that May and June in New York—what could Wolff send him? Wolff wrote that he was "fresh out of ideas."[9]

At the end of 1955 Feldman had written to Wolff and urged him to "spread the gospel—write articles and wait." Wolff complied with the admonition via Stockhausen, who asked Wolff for an article (in German) about Webern for his new journal, *Die Reihe*, the house organ for the Darmstadt summer courses, a pan-European musical curriculum touting the latest "researches" in composition. In summer 1956, as Wolff headed home, he made a stopover in Darmstadt, where Feldman's teacher, Stefan Wolpe, and Tudor both held forth, giving hasty surveys of new American developments, including Wolff's *For Piano I* and *For Piano II*. After Tudor played the pieces, a young Harvard student composer and pianist, Frederic Rzewski, approached Wolff, introduced himself, and arranged to pursue common interests in experimental music back at Harvard, where Rzewski, though he considered Randall Thompson his best teacher, was also known as the first person to acquire the latest radical scores (even before the university library).[10] In the fall, Rzewski introduced Wolff to a younger friend, David Behrman, now president of the Harvard undergraduate music club. That gave Behrman and, in turn, Rzewski and Wolff, rent-free access to Paine Hall for recitals. They scheduled a joint performance of experimental music for the spring semester.

But Wolff, now beginning a graduate program in comparative literature, had acquired a teaching assistantship with a massive load. For just one of the two classes he taught in spring semester, for example, he had to teach *Don Quixote*, *Gulliver's Travels*, *Tom Jones*, *Great Expectations*, *Moby-Dick*, and *War and Peace*—all, of course, major works outside of the canon of his undergraduate studies. He had little time to compose, at least not the kind of elaborate, precisely notated scores he had already produced. The question he faced then was how to achieve an elaborate post-Webernesque musical surface that was structured and had a sheen of virtuosic intensity but did not require labored composition, let alone practice, of the intricate rhythms and complex chords he favored. He decided to move toward some kind of indeterminate notation in a new piano duo that allowed himself and Rzewski latitude, not improvisation per se (with which they had little experience), but which freed them from the dictates of a rigorously determinate score. At the same time, an ingrained desire to break new ground with each work impelled Wolff to devise notations different from any he had yet seen.

In 1950 Feldman had written the first of his *Projections* pieces, which began several years of "box notation," in which pitch was governed only by register (high/middle/low) and intensity left completely indeterminate. Some of the pieces Earle Brown assembled into his *Folio* set (1952–53) consisted of notations that sometimes differed little from local visual artists' pen-and-ink drawings. In a way Brown had reached the very heart of the notational conundrum: what is the connection between sight and sound in the making of music? So long as the visual stimuli provoke an interesting aural result, Brown implicitly answered, the score, even if indeterminate in all parameters, still succeeds.[11]

However prescient he was in experimentalist construction of materials, though, Wolff had resisted experiments with notation. Except for his three-voice piece *Madrigals* (1950), which notated rhythm strictly but left pitch only relative, Wolff used only standard scoring techniques before 1957. In that year, for the prospective spring-semester, Wolff constructed a piece as he often had before, using small collections of pitches and clock-time schematics, all coupled with the extended techniques of the Cowell-Cage tradition, playing directly on the strings—harmonics, plucking, muting, and inserting preparations. Also, as one had come to expect in his scores, Wolff built substantial silences into each part, silences that, as in eighteenth-century counterpoint, the other player would likely fill. But Wolff went on to set up possibilities from which players had to choose in the course of playing. So, for example, one might have five seconds to play two pitches from a given collection. One could play them in either order, simultaneously, hold them for different durations, and so forth. This was, in concept, what he had done in determinate fashion in his first pieces (and not far from what one could choose to do in the box-notation pieces of Feldman).

For this piece, now discarded, Wolff developed a ratio system of notation that would characterize his next few pieces. Rather than *notes*, one might call these inscriptions *neumes*, signs for actions to take place but not specific sounds to be made. These earliest neumes in what would become Wolff's distinctive scores we call ratio neumes: each action has a numeric ratio. The first number in the ratio refers to a duration in seconds. The second number in the ratio refers to how many of a given group of pitches (or pitches chosen ad lib by the performer) to play. Modifications to the numbers (various letters and brackets) tell how to modify the pitches (e.g., transpose, prepare the strings) or the playing (i.e., inside-the-piano techniques).

Wolff was delighted at the result: "It made a music that, as far as sound went, was just as intricate and interesting as the stuff that we were making when we wrote everything out. This was a revelation. An enormous amount of this labor-intensive process of making every single note, every notation and so forth, which would take weeks or months, suddenly in twenty-four hours we had made a piece which worked like this, and which . . . was immediately available for performance."[12] Wolff was drawn to the efficiency of the process but also to the sense of controlled improvisation to which it led. It was not free, really, but rather a dialogue between two equally equipped players who would respond to each other with choices necessarily conditioned by what the other played. And that interaction enlivened the piece perhaps more than if the parts had been carefully constructed and strictly dictated to the players by the composer. In this piece, Wolff had reconciled with his early interest in Dixieland jazz—not overtly, he says, but subliminally. "It's like a chord chart," he said, a "funny version of a chord chart. And you do riffs over it, with that material."[13]

That piano duo became the prototype for Wolff's next four pieces, each for one or more pianos, each with verbal instructions longer than the one preceding it, and all scored with ratio neumes. The first of these pieces was probably the Sonata for Three Pianos, premiered in April 1957.[14] Asked to write for a concert of multiple piano works, Wolff devised this relatively simple work, with no score but three individual piano parts, not coordinated except that durations must be followed strictly enough (preferably using stopwatches) that the players proceed at the same pace and end at the same time. The Sonata used a kind of baseline notation, derived from the earlier prototype, on which all later works of this type would elaborate: simple ratios denoting time on the left and number of sounds on the right, pitch collections from which to choose, preparations for certain notes carefully specified, and a few dynamics scattered throughout. As with all of the ratio-neume pieces, the tiny fractional time values could be extraordinarily difficult to manage. But there was no inside-the-piano playing in the sonata, nor was there any cuing among players. Although strikingly new, even in the experimental context of this recital, Wolff disliked the sonata and spoke to Feldman about revising it. Feldman suggested he just proceed differently in his next piece.

That piece, Duo for Pianists 1, again had no full score, only a part for each player. The notation resembled that of the sonata but now prescribed some silences (i.e., with a "0" on the right of the ratio sign), allowed for some ad lib octave transpositions, and occasionally called for playing inside the piano. Preparations were no longer prescribed; rather, each performer chose two different preparations to be assigned to notes more or less ad lib. Although Wolff had the parts ready only a week before the concert, Tudor and Cage premiered it at Harvard, ten days before Christmas 1957. As it turned out, both performers ended up translating the new notation into "normal" notation on regular score paper, making the various choices ahead of the performance and then practicing them in a relatively conventional way. "The more choices [Wolff] offered," Tudor explained, "the more it was necessary to write it out. . . . When you have twenty-four different pitches you can choose from and it doesn't make any difference to him what they are—the point is, it makes a difference to *you.* It's a possibility that he didn't think of, that it would make a difference to the performer."[15]

There is no way (and perhaps no need) to tell how "accurate" that premiere performance was. But we can deduce the general effect of the piece. As with other Wolff pieces, the gestures echoed Webern's pithiness and understatement. Yet the new notation gave the piece a particular character, mentally focused yet playful. It provided a solid answer to Darmstadt serialism, which had begun to produce highly determinate, ultraorganized scores that Wolff thought aesthetically dead. His intent, born of the exigencies of graduate work in another discipline, was to make a score that would be less text than pretext for musical conversation, yet with a clear affection for the atomized sonorities he admired in Webern.

The Duo for Pianists 1, like the two pieces before it, energized Wolff. He had now learned to write pieces that were about music making, not "music" (and certainly not pitch, which Boulez insisted was the most important element of music). In the duo, Wolff effectively demoted pitch in the hierarchy of musical values by allowing players to choose pitches from groups he gave them.[16] The quality of surprise that gives pleasure to repeated performances of a work had grown tremendously through his new notation. Still, these works raised questions. Some were practical. How could one accurately execute the complex time lengths? (Cage and Tudor had used stopwatches in performance to maintain at least a semblance of synchronicity.) How should a performer judiciously make decisions about pitch, register, and various special effects? Other questions were more philosophical. What is the identity of the piece? How far can one rely on performers' good faith when one leaves them so many choices? As it turned out, the difficulty of these questions only added to the sense of mystery that tantalized Wolff and his New York School colleagues.

Wolff expanded on these questions in the Duo for Pianists II (1958). In this work for unprepared pianos, Wolff for the first time allowed for a "0" to be placed on the *left* side of a ratio, meaning any amount of time or even no amount of time. He also conceded that some tones could extend beyond their given time. Most important, the coordination of events in Duo II depended on elaborately described cues, the idea of which, Wolff explained, derived partly from Indian musical "games" in which players must listen to each other to determine what to play next.

Here is a simple explanation of how these cues work. Placed in a circle before almost every section of events is a particular type of sound (e.g., "high *ff*"). Whatever type a player last heard performed by the other player dictates which section or sections to play next. Thus, when player 1 hears a high, very loud pitch played by player 2, he or she must play a passage marked with that cue ("high *ff*") on his or her score. That means that not only must each player be prepared to go to any portion of the piece based on choices the other makes, but also that the piece had no fixed length: cues keep propelling it forward, ad infinitum. In this work, cues always trumped time, because the playing, Wolff said, had to remain continuous and there was no cue for ending. It was a kind of Möbius strip of material, with the ending delegated either to the performers' prearrangement of approximate clock-time length or their ad lib decision to stop. Thus the piece shifted the music's premises even further away from sound or even time—heretofore the foundation of Wolff's musical structuring—into the realm of relationships.

It was perhaps inevitable that such a piece would be both overrehearsed and underrehearsed. On one hand a player had to prepare for many possibilities, many contingencies beyond those an ordinary performance demanded. There was no fixed set of demands to which one must remain true. That situation required preparation above and beyond "normal" rehearsal. On the other hand, one simply could not prepare for as many possibilities as one might encounter or rehearse any one of them as many times as one would need to accommodate any contingency. The tension that ensues seemed unnerving—or perhaps *nerving* in the sense that each player in the Duo II had to be fully present in the moment of performance. One could not "lose oneself" in the piece but only stay alert for the piece's constant mutations.

When Cage and Tudor premiered it at Darmstadt in September 1958 (alongside Duo I, both pieces in multiple versions), many listeners found the piece boring, Cage said.[17] But he felt it accomplished a higher intellectual aim than sonic pleasure or mental play. In it, Cage said, "a thing which is difficult to rationally conceive takes place, namely zero time."[18] "Have you ever noticed how you read a newspaper? Jumping around, leaving articles unread, or only partially read, turning here and there. Not at all the way one reads Bach in public, but precisely the way one reads in public *Duo II for Pianists* by Christian Wolff."[19] In that work Cage believed his former student had moved music's substance from object to process. Duo II was "evidently not a time-object, but rather a process the beginning and ending of which are irrelevant to its nature."[20] "You see," said Cage, "if music is conceived as an *object*, then it has a beginning, middle, and end, and one can feel rather confident when he makes measurements of the time. But when [music] is *process* [as in Duo II], those measurements become less meaningful, and the process itself, involving if it happened to, the idea of Zero Time (that is to say no time at all), becomes mysterious and therefore eminently useful."[21] Cage later explained such "usefulness" by suggesting that only mystery makes art truly useful for changing one's thinking, which was art's ideal purpose.[22]

Although Wolff avoided conscription in France, by the spring of 1959 he could no longer do so in the United States, not because he was ineligible for deferment, but because he had forgotten to send the draft board his annual student exemption papers on time. So in the spring of 1959, claiming conscientious objector status, he entered the service as a noncombatant. On 11 June 1959 Wolff began his army service, arriving at Fort Sam Houston in San Antonio for training as a medic. During that month and the next he completed the next piece in his evolving cycle of piano works. Though he generically titled it *For Pianist*, Wolff specifically meant it for Tudor, not only to challenge the virtuoso, but in fact to disrupt his normal working methods. Tudor always rescored indeterminate pieces in order to practice them.[23] This piece would frustrate such attempts.

As with the two duos, Wolff used ratio notation and inside-the-piano playing (without preparations). But many aspects were new. Some pitch choices were now completely open—that is, with no arrays of notes from which to choose. Wolff for the first time included fermatas. And the pages may be played in any order (an idea Wolff borrowed from pieces by Brown and Stockhausen). What may be most striking (and daunting) new aspect of the piece is the remaking of the two hands into a veritable "duo," functioning somewhat independently, with hand-crossings being choreographed diagrammatically. Wolff adapted the cuing technique of Duo II to a solo performer: the player had to respond to cues created by the possible outcomes of what the player already attempted—how long or loudly a struck note sounded, whether a harmonic was accurately played, and so on. Different outcomes required the player to play different responses. This created a new kind of virtuosity for the methodical Tudor. He had to attempt a hyperconsciousness of each moment, yet reacting not to another player's choices but to the unforeseen consequences of his own. In this way, the piece continued in a deepening track for Wolff: the music was less about the sounds it produced than about the method of executing them. "That piece was terribly frustrating," Tudor would later confess. "But the music was beautiful."[24]

The culmination of Wolff's ratio-neume notation came in his next work, a chamber piece written during his first summer as an enlisted man: *Music for Six or Seven Players* (also known simply as *Music for Merce Cunningham*). This was his second work for Cunningham, director of New York's premiere experimental dance company, for which Wolff would write intermittently over the next six decades. Wolff had met Cunningham shortly after meeting his partner, Cage, in 1950 and received a commission—his first—from Cunningham in 1952. That resulted in his one nonpiano piece of that period, *Music for Magnetic Tape I*, on which Wolff had collaborated with Ted Schulz, an engineering student at Harvard, gathering and recording sounds, and then fully notating them into a score, with sound sources and durations (in inches, at 15" per second) for each layer of sound. Cage, Brown, Tudor, and others then assembled the piece, cutting the tape from the specified source and splicing it to the next sound source (or silence) for each of up to five tracks, which were then overdubbed. *Music for Magnetic Tape I* became the basis for Cunningham's dance titled *Suite by Chance*, the first work in his repertory he had structured entirely using chance procedures (an idea he got from Cage). The music, though, disappointed Cunningham's dancers. Carolyn Brown, Earle's wife, found Wolff's sounds relentlessly harsh, noting that the rather gentle young composer himself seemed disquieted at what he had produced.[25]

Though that piece felt abrasive to the dancers, in 1957 Cunningham choreographed Wolff's Suite for Prepared Piano into an astonishing solo for himself, which he took on tour that year to great acclaim. Cunningham gave Wolff a second commission in the spring of 1959, this time for a twenty-five-minute chamber work, whose time divisions—from fifteen to ninety seconds apiece—Cunningham worked out and sent to Wolff. Wolff essentially patched the work together during free time at the army base, sending segments and instructions to Cage and Cunningham along the way—including the direction that Tudor should use some of *For Pianist* as a solo section in the new work. But in this work the complexity of ratio-neume notation began to reach a point of diminishing returns. Rzewski, who had spent the previous school year as a student of Milton Babbitt at Princeton, immediately got to study the new piece from his new post as Cunningham's rehearsal pianist. He was blunt about the problems he saw: Wolff had "created situations of too extreme difficulty—e.g. $\frac{1}{6}''$:2 with 40 or 50 possibilities—so that the fact that there is no time to *think*, but only time to perform mechanical operations, not only makes any freedom for the performer in such cases impossible, but also makes the liberties you allow him superfluous & therefore vain, since they cannot be fulfilled. (Otherwise it looks beautiful)." He added that the "possibilities" Wolff had proposed with any neume "in reality . . . do not exist: only one possibility exists, namely that which the performer has learned by rote."[26] He continued in a subsequent letter to critique the resultant sounds of these recent scores. Having heard *Music for Six or Seven Players* (called *Rune* on Cunningham's dance programs) four times thus far, Rzewski wrote Wolff: "With each piece your music becomes less plastic, more like a bizarre geometrical shape which is unrecognizable like a Moebius band, more disturbing as a result.—& this piece is the most disturbing."[27] The frozen, constellationlike pointillism of Webern continued to resound in Wolff's music, undoing, perhaps, the sense of free play that delegating choices to performers seemed bent on ensuring. As with *Music for Magnetic Tape I*, Wolff also faced criticism for this as dance music, though in at least one instance for reasons completely opposite from the earlier criticisms: it was not that the new work was harsh but that "the *pointillistic* score of Christian Wolff so *sparsely* sustained the pulse and breadth of the solo."[28]

British composer and pianist Cornelius Cardew played in the premiere of *Music for Six or Seven Players* as a concert work in Cologne, January 1960. He would soon write about the great promise he found in the score's seeming "impossibilities," wherein a player might have to execute numerous sounds or actions within a fraction of a second—or no seconds at all (the "zero time" that pleased Cage in Duo II). Wolff had made a score that "is no longer a notation that one can *read*. . . . it must be translated into a notation," often from some "impossible" constraints. The problem was to determine which among potentially conflicting "rules" in the notation took precedence or which were binding, which not.[29] Wolff's call for the playing of three notes in *zero* seconds, for example—not just a fraction of a second—led Cardew to remark that "groping for the ungraspable is the most satisfying of modern pastimes, where the satisfaction lies in the fact that satisfaction is impossible."[30]

But the sense of liberating process for which Wolff would become best known had not yet arrived. As he wrote to Cunningham in sending the parts to *Music for Six or Seven Players,* Wolff was beginning to suspect that he had "lost sight of the conditions of performance" in his music.[31] It was amid his new team-oriented military environs—which fortuitously hampered his access to a piano—that Wolff decided to completely revamp his notational practice in order to allow for more of the "possibilities" the ratio-neume pieces had ultimately obstructed. By the time he finished his military tour of duty, April 1961, his new scores would lean almost wholly away from structure toward applied sociology.

3 Vast, Sparse Areas of Possibility: 1960–1969

ALTHOUGH TRAINED AS A MEDIC in Texas, Wolff had been assigned in January 1960 to the Information Section of Headquarters, Seventh Army, in New York, from which he was shipped out to Patch Barracks, Stuttgart-Vaihingen, Germany, to become an instructor and administrative assistant, teaching officers and enlisted men how to teach and managing paperwork for servicemen at all levels. The director of the schools, Burdette Stampley, would later write glowingly of how "cooperative, imaginative and highly intelligent in every respect" he found Wolff in planning, teaching, and indeed being "the epitome of tact" in working with his military students.[1] At the same time, Wolff developed his musicianship through prose polemics and new compositional strategies.

In 1960 Stockhausen's *Die Reihe* published a second article by Wolff. Moving from a detailed discussion of Cage's square-root form, through summaries of music by Earle Brown and Stockhausen, Wolff uses his own Duo II as a case study in "precise actions under various indeterminate conditions." He explains how form might be detached from older notions of "structure" and become simply "a theatrical event [whose] length itself may be unpredictable." In so doing, he calls into question the form-determining character of a score. "The score makes no finished object, at best hopelessly fragile or brittle. There are only parts which can be at once transparent and distinct."[2]

Around this time Wolff began dropping ratio neumes from his scores in favor of what we might call coordination neumes—lines with circles attached, angled variously to indicate interactions among players. In the Duet I (December 1960) for piano 4 hands, his first work to use this notation, two pages of score accompany three pages of explanation. As in *For Pianist,* Wolff uses lettered pitch gamuts from which the performer must choose, specifies various inside-the-piano techniques, and governs the progress of the piece by cues. The two pages of the score should be played in order—*or* only one of the two pages may be played. Many pitches are given with a threefold range of durations:

filled notehead = shortest to medium
square open notehead = medium to very long
ovular open notehead = any duration

Meanwhile, the eight different coordination neumes include symbols for

attack as simultaneously as possible, but player 2 holds longer than 1
1 starts anytime, 2 plays as soon as possible after 1 releases
2 plays first, then 1 and both release together

and so forth. In this way, Wolff continued to develop style traits he had shown as early as his teenage violin duo, where different relationships of starting and ending interacted with the compulsive restriction of pitch. In this new duet, strategies of listening and reacting trump pitch and rhythm as the fundamental structuring principles of the work, which has no implicit duration, only the instruction to "end when neither player wants to go on." But on a larger level, the score demands the relearning of what a "score" is. The rules are clear, painstakingly so, but so detailed and often intricate that they resemble rules one might find in sophisticated board games.

Wolff used variations of this kind of notation (with occasional ratio neumes added back in) in other schematically notated and generically named pieces written while he served in the army (through April 1961) and in the summer months thereafter, during which he attended the University of Munich: Suite II (horn and piano), Duet II (horn and piano), Trio II (piano 4 hands, percussion), Duo for Violinist and Pianist, and finally, the most complex of the lot, *Summer* for string quartet (August 1961). After that work, Wolff would take a year hiatus from composition while he worked on his dissertation and taught again at Harvard.

Meanwhile, he began to get his previous work published and recorded. In November 1960, Walter Hinrichsen of the C. F. Peters music publishing company made a deal with Wolff to publish all of Wolff's music, an arrangement similar to one Peters had just made with Cage. (At this time, Cage had published his first book of essays, *Silence*, in which he had named Wolff prominently as a mentor for his ideas.) What Peters had not bargained for was the difficulty of engraving Wolff's new notations. Eventually, offset versions of Wolff's manuscripts and typed instructions proved the only feasible means of publishing them. At the same time, the small independent label Time Records hired Earle Brown to produce a series of new music albums anthologizing the most radical new music in Europe and the United States. The series, which ran from 1961 to 1963 (reissued on the Mainstream label, 1970), included recordings of works by over two dozen composers, including Stockhausen, Luciano Berio, Henry Cowell, Charles Ives, and Brown's New York School peers—Cage, Feldman, and Wolff.

The next threshold in Wolff's experimental evolution came in 1962, when he began a two-year span of writing only pieces with unspecified instrumentation. The first was *For 5 or 10 Players*, whose ensemble could consist of any five or ten performers (nothing in between), each player using one of the ten score pages (or two of the ten in the version for five players). Although instrumentation remained open, the notation geared the choices away from instruments with limited timbres because so many of this piece's neumes required timbral changes. The spare notation represented a multivalent system in which one had to learn new rules for how to construe simple arabic numerals (in the same way that, in more conventional notation, a "3" could represent a fingering, the top of a time signature, or a triplet).

For a sense of the work's demands (i.e., possibilities), consider the first page of its score, seen in figure 2. Each inverted U shape (which we'll call a cap for convenience) represents a sonic event. An event generally consists of two parts: event material (how many sounds and what kind) and event coordination (when to begin and when to end). The event material appears above the coordination material; a vertical bracket connecting capped events gives the player the option of executing either event. The first things notated under each cap are pitch and timbre: a number in a box tells the number of pitches to be played; an unboxed number represents the number of timbres to be played; no boxed number means only one pitch, no unboxed number means only one timbre; an x in either position allows the player to choose. Thus (using letters we have added to fig. 2) the page shows the following:

A = 1 pitch, 4 timbres
B = 1 pitch, 1 timbre
C = 2 pitches, 3 timbres
D = 1 pitch, 2 timbres
E = 1 pitch, 1 timbre

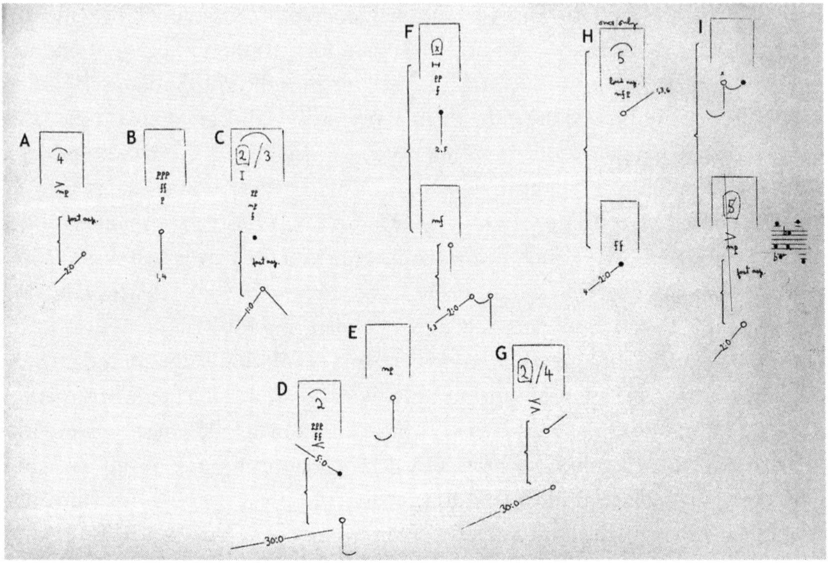

Figure 2. The first page of the score to *For 5 or 10 Players* (with added letters for identifications). Peters EP 6637. Used by permission of Peters Edition, Ltd.

F = any number of pitches, 1 timbre *or* 1 pitch, 1 timbre
G = 2 pitches, 4 timbres
H = 1 pitch, 5 timbres *or* 1 pitch, 1 timbre
I = 1 pitch, 1 timbre *or* 5 pitches from the set shown, 1 timbre

The next level beneath each cap shows dynamics, with another set of rules. On the lowest level beneath each cap Wolff has coordination neumes, which show how many seconds before or after others sounds an event should be executed (as in earlier compositions for specified instruments). All the levels of notation for events suggest a complex interlocking of actions and reactions to be learned and planned.

After *For 5 or 10 Players*, Wolff wrote his next three pieces with similarly free instrumentation: *In Between Pieces* (1963), and 1964's Septet and *For 1, 2 or 3 People*. The sketches for the latter, seen in figure 3, suggest how much Wolff had moved from the hyperspecific timings and pitch collections of his work in the 1950s to a concern with relationships between "people" (the shift from "players" in the earlier work's title to "people" is instructive).

The finished composition streamlined and simplified the scoring of *For 5 or 10 Players*, making it easier to perform and requiring less conscious "thinking" while playing, see table 1.

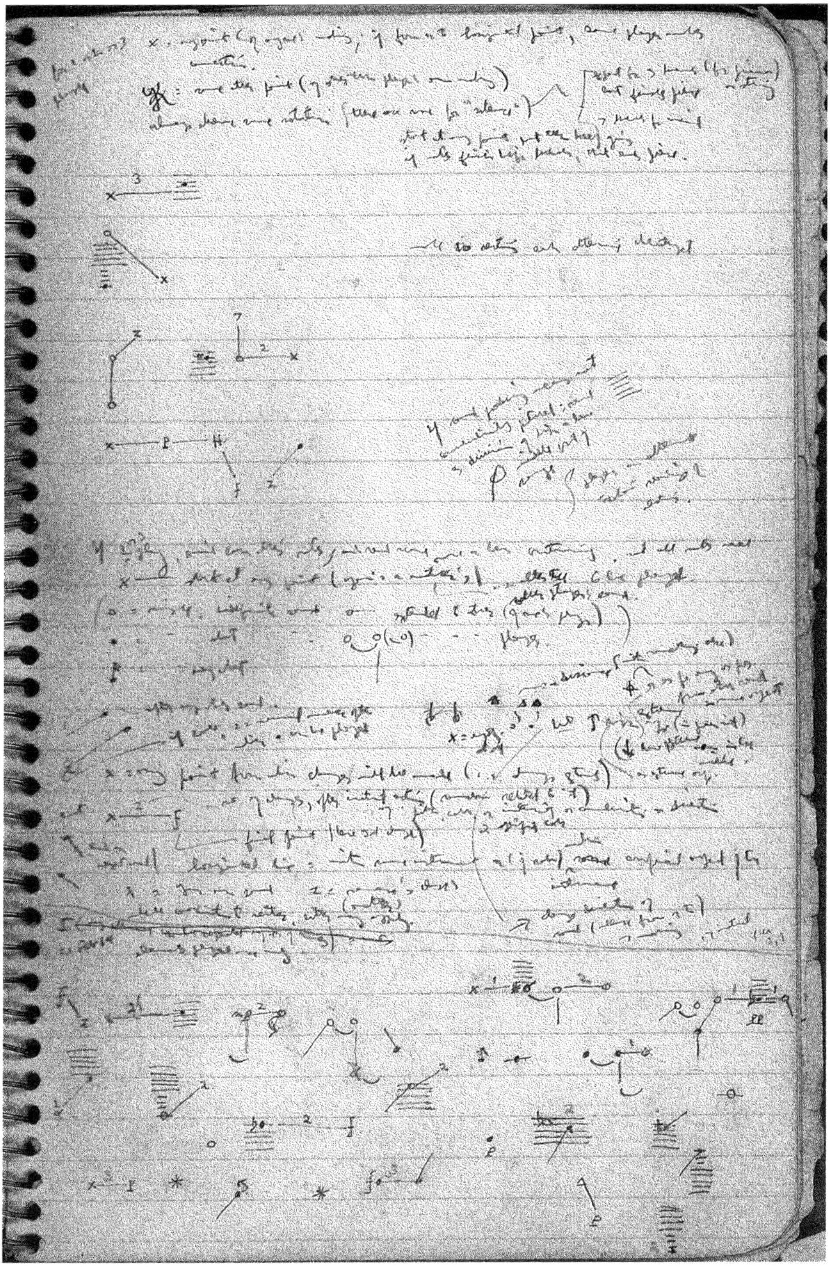

Figure 3. A page from Wolff's sketches for *For 1, 2 or 3 People.* Wolff Papers. Used by permission.

Comparison of Score Layout and Performance Logistics in For 5 or 10 Players *and* For 1, 2 or 3 People

For 5 or 10 Players 10 pages	*For 1, 2 or 3 People* 10 pages
5-person version: players can have either one page (1–5 or 6–10), two pages (a = 1&6, b = 2&7, c = 3&8, etc.), or each player gets a copy of all ten pages 10-person version: each player gets one page unique to him or her, or two pages (a&b = 1&6, c&d = 2&7, etc.), or each player gets a copy of all ten pages.	The group chooses which page (or pages) to play. Each player has a copy of this page (or these pages). They all divide the events on the page(s) between members of the ensemble (i.e., players may not share events). Division is specified for two players on page 7; they perform the chosen page(s) together.
At any time during the course of a performance, the entire ensemble, on cue, performs all of the events on their pages in sequence, left to right. At other times, the players may play any events in any sequence from their pages, unless the events themselves constrain order or repetition.	All events must be played, in any order, and may not be repeated. The exception is page 9, which allows omissions and repetitions.
Complicated coordinations, with many rules	The coordination neumes are simpler. Events do not use "caps" or brackets.
(Solo performance is not an option)	The possibility of solo performance presents unique challenges. Wolff suggests coordination between events when possible, or coordination with environmental sounds.
Large numbers at the top of events: boxed number = number of pitches (if no boxed number, then one pitch) Unboxed number = number of timbres (if no number, then one timbre)	Black numbers = number of pitches (no number given = 1) Red numbers = number of timbres (no number given = 1) A number on a coordination line = that number of changes in some aspect(s) of the sound if black, or timbre if red, during the course of the coordination. A red 1 = a different timbre from the immediately preceding one

The smaller numbers of personnel it required also made it more practical and portable than *For 5 or 10*, especially since a solo performer could execute it. The piece caught on, especially through Rzewski, who had been living in Europe since 1963 and mounted performances of *For 1, 2 or 3* in several countries, leading him to write Wolff in November 1964 that his parts to the piece were "already used up."[3]

During the time he was composing *For 1, 2 or 3*, Wolff provided a brief but highly concentrated explanation of his motives for such scoring. In an interview published in the Palermo journal *Collage*, Wolff explained that his philosophical aim was "to have made something hazardous with which we may try ourselves," a kind of précis for the idea of "danger music" that would become a cause célèbre in some experimental circles. His task as a composer was to deploy "fixed points" around which performers could move. Wolff explained how he arrived at such a task in terms that were at once mundane and radical. To compose this way was quicker. It avoided redundancy in performances. It made the music better able to accommodate "interference" or "contingencies" in performance. Perhaps most important, the new notation led to a psychosonoric effect in which a listener could perceive "the sound of a player making up his mind, or having to change it."[4]

By the time he wrote *For 1, 2 or 3*, Wolff's academic and family moorings had begun to shift. In January 1963, he submitted his 170-page dissertation for the doctorate in comparative literature. Titled "Aspects of the Later Plays of Euripides," it was a close reading of *Ion*, *Orestes*, and *Iphegenia Among the Taurians*, followed by an explication of common themes and motifs in the plays. But the introduction to the dissertation seemed to hint at aesthetic issues in Wolff's music. In the three plays Wolff found "a great variety of elements and qualities often shifting abruptly, contrary, sometimes violently opposed." And in the chapters that followed, he said, he would explore how Euripides's plots "demonstrate the negation of intended actions."[5] Wolff's music, of course, had increasingly devolved on actions and reactions leading to unforeseen consequences of subtle gestures. But while his attitude toward Euripides hinted at aesthetic themes in his music, Wolff's painstaking intellectual analysis reflected the stringency of methods by which he and his New York School colleagues often composed.

Kurt Wolff often traveled to Europe to visit family and scout for new authors. In October 1963, as he was walking in Ludwigsburg, Germany, a tanker truck backed into him, crushing him against a wall. He died three hours later. The publishing world lamented the loss of a literary pioneer whose Pantheon imprint had recently been sold to Random House. Helen carried on as an editor in her own right, championing the work of Karl Jaspers, Umberto Eco, Günter Grass, and other European authors via a new job at Harcourt Brace. Her reputation grew so much that by 1977 PEN would award her "For distinctive and continuous service to international letters, the freedom and dignity of writers and the free transmission of the printed word across barriers of repression, poverty, ignorance and censorship."[6]

On 1 August 1965, Cage and Tudor drove Jasper Johns's Jaguar to Vermont for a special occasion: on that day, with a new assistant professorship at Harvard now in hand, Christian married Hope ("Holly") Nash at St. Paul's Episcopal Church in Royalton. David Behrman played a small antique organ in the chapel.

The daughter of Ray Nash, a well-known art professor at Dartmouth, Holly had met Christian in the classics program at Harvard from which she had graduated summa cum laude (through Radcliffe) that June. She, like her new husband, had grown up in a musical home, though one entrenched in folk music, in which her mother, Hope, excelled. The next week, Holly left Royalton, her hometown, and helped Christian move out of his Claverly Hall room at Harvard and into an apartment in a modest old house on Sparks Street in Cambridge.

Now, as both a family man and Harvard classics professor, Wolff's path diverged even further from that of his friends John and Morty. In a 1966 series of one-on-one radio discussions, Cage and Feldman took stock of their relationship to Wolff and his work. Christian's early music particularly inspired Feldman, who said that if he looked at his own music from the 1950s, he found it "old hat": "It's

Figure 4. Holly Nash at her wedding to Christian Wolff (with Morton Feldman, left, behind her), 1 August 1965. Photographer unknown. Courtesy of Christian Wolff.

been around, it's been digested by myself [as if] having a bone on a plate and you forgot that you were chewing on it and you go back and you chew on it again, you know." But if one picked up a piece that Wolff wrote as teenager, one found that "there's certainly nothing old hat about it. . . . the whole continuity of the work, I mean, is just absolutely extraordinary. It's not musty, you're not opening up a tomb." One thing that kept Wolff's music fresh, Feldman added, was Christian's relative aloofness from the new music "scene," which allowed him to write piece after piece in logical steps without having to write sequels in his own presumptive "style." Feldman said, "I don't think my pieces would have been [old hat] if they weren't performed, if they weren't out in the world, so to speak." Cage agreed, adding that Wolff still had "that freedom that we have lost." He went on with a kind of peroration: "I think that that quality of classicism that was in Webern and which made his music useful for people who wanted to change their thinking about music exists now in the work of Christian Wolff. I found years ago that if one were teaching music and wanted to provide a discipline for a student that first one had to give up teaching harmony, next one had to give up teaching counterpoint. Now I think one would have to give up teaching Webern. And I think you'd be at the present moment a fairly good teacher if you would teach Christian Wolff['s] music to a student." Feldman heartily agreed: "I'm convinced that Christian is and will have the place of Webern in terms of the mind."[7]

Up until then, Wolff *as a performer* had been known only as a pianist, whether playing his own music, old-world classics (in his youth), or novelties (as in the Cage-produced marathon premiere performance of Satie's *Vexations* in September 1963). But Holly incited a new interest: the electric guitar. Nearly ten years younger than Christian, she introduced him to the music of rock groups, especially British Invasion favorites like the Beatles, the Rolling Stones, the Kinks, and the Who. Through their recordings he came to see the electric guitar not so much as the venerated six-stringed "queen of instruments" but as a highly flexible—and portable—electronic device. His fascination with the instrument led him to buy a low-priced Fender, which he played in a 1965 performance of *For 1, 2, or 3* that also featured Cage on bowed saw and Alvin Lucier on amplified bowed cymbal. After that appearance, Wolff composed his three *Electric Spring* pieces. The notation of these chamber works—his only compositions during 1966–67—foreshadowed much of what would follow in the 1970s: all instruments and most pitches were specified; durations were as in his recent pieces, except that now eighth and sixteenth notes were added to the repertoire of values; and there were no coordination neumes. Wolff played in the premieres of all three, with Holly playing electric bass in one of them.

Since 1965, David Behrman had been working as a tape editor on the swing shift at Columbia Masterworks. In the summer of 1967, Behrman asked his boss John McClure's permission to produce some of his friends' music for the label. McClure agreed, if Behrman could keep costs down. That November, the Columbia Records Group shocked Christmas buyers by issuing as its entire preholiday classical release seventeen titles, all from Behrman's new series or from older modernists like Stravinsky, Webern, and Ives.[8] Among them was the first release of a Wolff piece on a major label: *For 1, 2, or 3 People* played as a solo by David Tudor on an oddly prepared organ. Suddenly, the music of this obscure experimentalist was being marketed by the largest record company in the country. Within a month the first pressing of 1,500 copies had sold out.

But by then Wolff had left the States, taking a sabbatical from Harvard during the 1967–68 school year to live with Holly in London. There, Wolff immediately wrote to Cage, "the paperback of *Silence* is everywhere in the bookstore windows here, a kind of welcome."[9] Although Europe had often symbolized to Cage and his circle a recalcitrant orthodoxy of post-Webern serialism, the European-bred Wolff had always been able to find colleagues there who resonated to his brand of experimentalism. Rzewski helped: he had lived in Berlin 1963–66 and then moved to Rome, where he helped found MEV (Musica Electronica Viva), an electronic improvisational group. In England, that group mirrored an acoustic-electronic improvisational group called AMM (whose initials had a secret meaning), a group consisting of Keith Rowe, Lou Gare, Eddie Prévost, Laurence Sheaff, and its latest addition, Cornelius Cardew, the best-known and perhaps most energetic of the British experimental music scene.

Wolff inevitably gravitated to Cardew, who since 1958 had been programming, recording, and broadcasting performances of Wolff's compositions, then reviewing and theorizing about them in British musical journals. Although the two men had met in Cologne in 1960, their professional relationship flowered during Wolff's sabbatical, resetting his musical career in several ways.[10] First, he began to improvise in earnest, sitting in with AMM, playing on a newly purchased hollow-body bass, often laid flat on his lap like a keyboard, sometimes bowed or "prepared" with objects stuck between the strings (as Keith Rowe did with his guitar). Generally, AMM played free improvisations. But Cardew soon began to translate his experiences with AMM into notated scores. The first was *Tiger's Mind* (1967), a page of prose in two paragraphs ("Daypiece" and "Nightpiece"), which narrated a mythical tiger's interactions with a tree, the wind, someone named Amy, and various other aspects of his environment. (Wolff interpreted "the tree" at the work's premiere.) Its follow-up was *Schooltime Compositions*, essentially a collation of two dozen sketchy and suggestive pages of wildly diverse notations for a series of "tasks" (rarely specified as musical) that together constituted what Cardew called an opera, in the original meaning of the word ("works"). As with *Tiger's Mind*, Wolff performed in the premiere of *Schooltime Compositions*. He then wrote his own score for AMM: *Edges*.

Different from any previous work of his (and unique in his entire opus), *Edges* (for an undefined number and type of players) consisted entirely of twenty-five symbols scattered around a single page. The symbols, say the instructions, do not necessarily denote the sounds to be played as such, but rather "mark out a space or spaces, indicate points, surfaces, routes or limits" around or within which to play. Yet each symbol has its own definition: some refer to relative height of pitch, some to durations, some to articulations, some to coordinations, some to sonic characters (e.g., "bumpy," "intricate"), and so forth. Typically, one plays what each notation suggests once only, though in no fixed order. AMM premiered the work in May 1968, with Wolff, Rzewski, Michael Parsons, Howard Skempton, and John Tilbury also sitting in. Rzewski wrote to Wolff that summer that *Edges* was "a beautiful piece," though confessed that he himself had stayed with a single notation ("in the middle") throughout the whole performance.[11] The following summer, Rzewski had his students playing the piece at one of the United States's most conservative and prestigious summer programs: Tanglewood.

If *Edges* grew out of Wolff's work with AMM, another new genre of works grew from his guest lectureships in British art schools, which were at the time more or less the engines that propelled the counterculture of the United Kingdom. These schools, with their quirky mixtures of aesthetic and practical training for advanced high school or college students, proved more open than music departments to sonic experimentation. The students had varying musical backgrounds; some could read and play from traditional notation, but most could not. The students also had access to few instruments, usually guitars and makeshift percussion. All had voices.

During lectureships at art schools in Bath, Leicester, and Winchester—the latter arranged by a free-spirited student named Brian Eno—Wolff decided to involve students as performers, writing sets of prose instructions from which even the least musically literate could make sounds in an organized way with whatever means were available. Such prose scores were indeed in the air, from the terse verbal directions of Fluxus composers such as La Monte Young, George Brecht, and Yoko Ono in the early 1960s to the text pieces that Stockhausen wrote in the spring of 1968, the same months that Wolff was writing his. But what distinguished Wolff's pieces was that they lacked the theatricality of the Fluxus compositions and the conceptualism of Stockhausen's. Wolff's text scores (later gathered together as part of his set called *Prose Collection*) could be seen as the rules to sonic games. They specify certain sound-producing activities, but never specific pitches or rhythms, except, sometimes, in relation to others in the group.[12] Some pieces call for (or allow for) instrumental playing, but only such as could be played by anyone, trained or not. Scores dictated ways of playing and relative densities of sound, but little else. (The only "lyrics" appear in the pieces "Crazy Mad Love" and "Song," where the performers vocalize phrases and names for specified numbers of times.) Overall these scores might be described as exercises in following directions in a group—the nature of all ensemble scoring, to be sure, but in this case containing, in microcosm, much of Wolff's by now well-established intricacy of social relationships and mutual responses in performance. John Cage, when he saw some of them, said they were distillations of what had before been fully, if indeterminately, notated in Wolff's earlier scores. When five of these pieces were published together, Cardew reviewed the set for the *Musical Times* with predictable exuberance:

> With the conviction that the light embodied in this music should be diffused throughout the world and its source obliged to continue shining, since great changes would be wrought by a widespread awareness of this new and timeless music—*eg* what's rotten would disintegrate leaving our insight into Nature (including humanity) more penetrating and affectionate—a number of Wolff's English admirers subscribed towards the printing of this collection. . . . Embedded in the prose like the jewels in a watch mechanism are traces of the beautifully flexible musical notation that Wolff has evolved over the past 15 years, delineating vast, sparse areas of possibility with simple and articulate precision.[13]

But to Wolff personally, Cardew wrote, "I can't remember when I last heard such beautiful music."[14]

Although Harvard was his alma mater and the home of many of his early musical exploits, Wolff had not had the opportunity to teach music there. But with so much of his energy flowing into his composing, he failed to write and publish the kind of scholarly works the classics department demanded. So when he returned from England in the fall of 1968, he learned that his five-year teaching contract with Harvard would not be renewed. His British friends urged him to consider a post in England. Cage suggested that Wesleyan, where he now taught, might have an opening. But as 1969 began—just weeks before Christian and Holly's first child, Christian Mayhew ("Hew"), was born—a classics job opened up at Dartmouth. When Wolff went to interview, his father-in-law introduced him to Jon Appleton. At the age of twenty-nine, Appleton had just been appointed chair of the music department and was charged with improving the department's national stature. Since Wolff still entertained the divided loyalties that cost him the Harvard job, Lawrence Harvey, associate dean of faculty at Dartmouth, arranged to create a special appointment for Wolff in classics and music, with comparative literature—the field of Wolff's doctorate—thrown in. But the school needed letters of recommendation before an official hire. To that end, avant-garde composers from Stockhausen to Cage wrote on Wolff's behalf. Understandably glowing, Cage's letter included this statement:

> He is not known as a student of mine for the reason that I learned more from him than he from me. . . . Through the association of David Tudor, Morton Feldman, myself, and Christian Wolff, American music has developed to the point of shaping new music not only here but in the Orient and in Europe. This is generally acknowledged. It was because of this that last year I was made a member of the National Institute of Arts and Letters. It is only my age that has brought it about that I am so distinguished: the truer state would be that such honors go to Christian Wolff. For of the four of us, I am certain that his work is the most regenerative of music.[15]

Dartmouth hired Wolff and thereby at last codified the professional double life he had been leading for years: a scholar of old, canonized works, mostly in dead languages, and maker of heterodox works in newly invented languages.

Dartmouth itself had started to diverge in its personality: amid conservative politics and old-money society, it now pioneered computer technology, electronic (and digital) sound synthesis, and progressive courses that included black studies, environmental studies, Native American studies, and women's studies. A strong anti–Vietnam War faction began to grow among the newer, younger faculty brought in to meet the growth of the student body now that women were being admitted. With Wolff's appearance, the school would suddenly have an experimental composer teaching music in the Hopkins Center for the Arts and classics in Dartmouth Hall.

But Wolff had to wait before he could start at his new school. Because, despite having just been denied tenure at Harvard, he won in 1970 one of eight junior fellowships at the Harvard-affiliated Center for Hellenic Studies in Washington, D.C. In the fall of that year he moved with Holly and their two children—daughter Tamsen had been born that April—to one of the homes for residents at the center.[16] For nine months he worked on two projects in Washington: a new translation and commentary for Euripides' *Herakles* (per a contract with Prentice-Hall) and a study of Euripides' *Helen* (which would appear in a 1973 issue of *Harvard Studies in Classical Philology*).

Figure 5. Christian and son Mayhew in East Barnard, Vermont, ca. 1971. Photographer unknown. Courtesy of Christian Wolff.

In the summer of 1971, Holly's father, Ray Nash, retired from Dartmouth as she, Christian, Hew, and Tamsen arrived in Hanover, New Hampshire. They bought the Nash home on Main Street, and Ray moved with his wife, Hope, to their Royalton, Vermont, farm, where Holly had been born. Christian began preparing for classes and completing a large-scale work named for a hardy, tangled weed: *Burdocks*.

4 Let Playing Be Composition and Composition Playing: 1969–1974

IN JUNE 1969, AMID HIS NEGOTIATIONS with Dartmouth, Wolff had received a letter from John Tilbury inviting him to put money into—and even join—a new venture of Cardew's: the Scratch Orchestra, a quasi-anarchic group of trained and untrained musicians who would perform improvisatory new pieces and ad hoc renditions of conventional old ones.[1] The group would embody Cardew's "ethics of improvisation," which saw improvisation as a tool to develop virtue and strength through cooperation. "Training" (including "moral discipline") would replace "rehearsal," so that preparing for performance would not be like preparing a play so much as preparing to play a sport.[2] Beyond its idealism, the Scratch Orchestra had an air of novelty that enabled it to quickly publish its constitution in the *Musical Times*, begin booking concerts, and appear on radio and television within its first year.

In late 1968, Cardew had finished the first portion of what would be a basic score for the Scratch Orchestra: *The Great Learning*, a massive seven-part setting of the first chapter of Confucius's text by that name. Its notation varied with each section, though mostly used conventional symbols, but with some less-determinate sections and lots of verbal directions. The title summarized what Wolff and his art-school colleagues saw as the point of music now: education via new instructions.

Wolff explained this in a 1970 article that echoed both Cardew's "ethics" and Cage's embrace of all sounds.

> A composition (a score) is only material for performance: it must make possible the freedom and dignity of the performers; it should allow at any moment surprise, for all concerned, players, composer, listeners; it should allow both concentration, precision in detail, and release, or collapse, virtuosity and doing things in the ordinary way. No sound, noise, interval, et cetera as such is preferable to any other sound, including those always around us, provided that (a) one is free to move away or towards it, and that (b) sounds are not used deliberately to compel feelings in others; let the listeners be just as free as the players.[3]

As a venue for these ideals, the Scratch Orchestra tantalized Wolff. Although he couldn't yet travel to hear them, in the summer of 1970, before heading for the Center for Hellenic Studies, he began a new piece in the spirit of *The Great Learning*. That new piece—along with a small music festival Wolff first held in August 1969 on his father-in-law's Vermont farm—he titled *Burdocks.*

Written with the still-unheard Scratch Orchestra in mind, *Burdocks* was for "one or more orchestras"—though the work's performance notes redefined "orchestra" to mean as few as five players, yet allowed for as many as ten such orchestras to be playing at once. Sound sources were free, except where specific sounds (e.g., pitches) were needed. Its overall structure was open: no set number of movements need be played, movements could be played in succession, simultaneously or in any combination of overlaps. At the same time, an elective political process undergirded the piece: players were to "gather and decide" or "choose one or more representatives to decide" which sections to play and in what order. In totality it comprised a compendium of compositional possibilities Wolff had used before. But its patchwork quality also bespoke Wolff's familial status: having two young children in the home he now had to write more catch-as-catch-can, jotting down fragments and keeping himself as interruptible as possible.

Each movement of *Burdocks* had a distinct identity based on methods and techniques always slightly—or hugely—different from all others (* beside a number means that it contains graphic notation along with the verbal):

1. Five segments, primarily consisting of players responding to one another's pitches, articulations and dynamics in various ways.

2.* Somewhat loosely articulated block-chord segments. (Wolff thought of this as the "chorale" movement.)

3. Each player makes ca. 511 sounds, each different in some way.

4. Each player plays 1–3 soft sounds, coordinating them with every other player in succession.

5.* Six different multispoked wheels, with different kinds of musical gestures between each pair of spokes and different pathways from wheel to wheel. (Perhaps the most complicated movement in its notation.)

6.* A repeatable, anthemlike melody (built from smaller, self-similar fragments) with accompanimental gestures. (The melody is the most conventionally notated material in the set.)

7.* A graphic score that seems a radical splaying of the score of section 2 (above).

8.* 100 different short ideas, most on clefless staves, and all to be played once only.

9. A moderately elaborate plan for having players respond to one another's sounds; a gradual acceleration to the conclusion.

10. A single conceptualist prompt: "Flying, and possibly crawling or sitting still."

If the Scratch Orchestra provided an imaginary sonic and social model for some of the performative techniques of *Burdocks*, an African field recording inspired the new work's heterophonic textures. In the spring of 1970, Canadian composer Jack Behrens had invited Wolff for a brief residency at Simon Fraser University in Vancouver. In Behrens's office, Wolff encountered volume 3 of *An Anthology of African Music*, part of the elegantly produced UNESCO series of LPs featuring music from the Eastern Hemisphere. This LP consisted of fifteen tracks of Ba-Benzélé pygmy music: hunt songs, story-telling songs, laments, and entertainments, all with free, unmetered counterpoint and hocketing that sometimes alternated between singing and whistling.[4] The sound provided a fresh sonic model. It also gave Wolff, as a professor of comparative literature, a musical foundation squarely *outside* the Western canon. His music could now be "traditional," but from a different tradition.

Burdocks was a threshold. It was Wolff's first work intended for a large ensemble. It was his first multimovement work in which each movement had distinctly different instructions on how and what to play. And it was his longest in actual (not just conceptual) performance. With the Green Mountains as a backdrop, a sextet of Behrman, Rzewski, Tudor, Gordon Mumma, Wolff, and his brother-in-law, John Nash, premiered five movements of *Burdocks* at the second Burdock Festival in mid-August 1971 at the Nash farm in Royalton, Vermont. The quintet then traveled to Dartmouth to record the movements for a record to be issued on the Wergo label. A slightly different quintet (which included Dartmouth colleague Jon Appleton) played *Burdocks* excerpts the following January at New York University to a small audience that included Cage and Cunningham, the latter of

Figure 6. The cover to the UNESCO recording that influenced Wolff in ideas of hocket and heterophony. Courtesy of Brigham Young University Recording Archive.

whom soon used the piece for a new dance, *Borst Park*. Meanwhile, on 9 September 1971, Cardew had written to Wolff, apologizing for not being able to attend the Vermont quasi premiere of *Burdocks* but promising to program the work with the Scratch Orchestra, in part to help them weather some growing dissent in the ensemble: "We have had massive upheavals & Burdocks will bring us together again for lots of work and pleasure."[5]

What were those cryptic "upheavals"? In the summer of 1971, Cardew had led a faction of the Scratch Orchestra in reading and discussing Mao's lengthy three-decade-old Yenan Forum speech on proletarian art. The following January, he and other Scratch members had become dogmatic that the orchestra must shun the bourgeois trappings of the professional musical world, including even its avant-garde fringes. When he programmed *Burdocks* for the Scratch Orchestra's next concert, the group angrily divided, most hard-core Maoists finding Wolff's piece "contentless," lacking in political relevance and mass appeal. But Cardew surprisingly defended the piece, insisting that they play *Burdocks* and give the audience the right to decide its worth. After weeks of wrangling, the group played it on 28 March 1972, giving *Burdocks* its first complete, large-ensemble realization. Indeed, they made a whole evening event of it, with over sixty people playing the ten sections not once but twice, introduced by Cardew's own political polemic (including the defense he had made of the piece to his Maoist colleagues) and the two versions separated by a discussion and a few songs. The second playing of the piece included the younger working class's sonic foundation: electric guitars at rock-concert decibel levels.

Shortly before that performance, Hans Keller of the BBC Music Section asked Cardew to write about John Cage for the *Listener* magazine to prepare readers for a series of Cage concerts planned for that summer. Cardew turned in a savage indictment he titled "John Cage: Ghost or Monster?" Taking the title from bourgeois types referred to in Mao's Yenan Forum talks, Cardew branded Cage an imperialist composer purveying a music without content. He analyzed (and mocked) pieces by Cage and ended his essay with a challenge: "It may not be all plain sailing, but there's no reason why [Cage] can't shuffle his feet over to the side of the people and learn to write music which serves their struggles."[6]

When Cardew sent Wolff a copy of the article, Christian and Holly discussed it for hours, making notes on how to respond to it. Cardew's polemic not only overreached, they concluded, but was "a model of harshness" with "distortions" and "over-simplifications" throughout. Wolff admitted he was troubled by Cage's separation of politics from "life." But even in a Marxist worldview, he found models for brilliant individualism. Above all, Wolff wanted "freedom"—including *individual* freedom—as an ideal that music could portray without text or vernacular affectations.[7]

He now found himself having to choose between two friends and mentors. While Cage had taught Wolff the unity of music and experiential life, Cardew had fused political life to that unity. All three men had come to admire Mao's teachings. But Cage resisted preaching them through music. Cardew, on the other hand, now took them so seriously that he began to reject his own earlier work, the elitism of the avant-garde generally, and Wolff's mentor in particular.[8] Wolff looked for a middle path that honored both friends but allowed him to move decisively toward political music, which he was beginning to feel was an imperative.[9]

Christian took until July to write back to Cardew. He thanked Cardew for the Scratch Orchestra's performance of *Burdocks* and for championing the piece despite its seemingly elitist origins. Wolff agreed that music should be for the people, but cited Rzewski that "music for the people is music in which the people participate." If the title, text, or context of a piece held political messages, the music could only be accompaniment: he couldn't imagine what "revolutionary character" music could have outside of that. He thought Cardew's attack on Cage "harsh" but also "harshly clear and so very useful." Cage disappointed him, he said, by attacking capitalism's brutality in his prose while downplaying potentially political aspects of music in favor of the merely social. Wolff liked Cardew's idea that one cannot straddle the question of politics—anything less than activism was obstructionism. But he questioned two of Cardew's conclusions. First, how can one be certain one has chosen the right political *cause*? And second, did music always have to be, as Cardew put it, "hard hitting and tough"? "Could it also be infiltrating, insinuating, subversive?"[10]

A week after writing that letter, Wolff was in Europe lecturing at the center place of the elitist avant-garde composition Cardew denounced: Darmstadt, where on 28–30 July 1972 Wolff lectured in English and German for two hours each afternoon.[11] The first U.S. composer invited to speak there since Milton Babbitt in 1964, Wolff tread a fine line, promoting the inherent collectivism of his open scores, but not condemning the high-art traditions that had nurtured his work, traditions notably represented by Iannis Xenakis, who preceded him a week earlier at Darmstadt; György Ligeti, who spoke concurrently with Wolff; and Stockhausen, who spoke the week following. Still, to many at the summer school, Wolff's relaxed outlook gave a new freshness and openness, an antidote to the formalism and structural obsessiveness for which the school had become known, especially in the fourteen years since Cage and Tudor had appeared there and played Wolff's duos.

The competing ideologies of Cage and Cardew erupted at a performance of *Burdocks* on Westdeutscher Rundfunk radio—Cardew's old employer—when both the Scratch Orchestra and John Cage were scheduled for the cultural program of the Munich Olympics at the end of August 1972. The Scratch Orchestra played *Burdocks* only after an introduction by Cardew with a Maoist attack on avant-garde "imperialism." That irritated Cage, Feldman, and Tudor, who also had an array of complaints about the orchestra's rendition, from a general lack of energy to the reading of a poem in the last section. One portion of the performance actually drove Feldman to his feet in protest. In *Burdocks*' fifth section, as a response to the isolated number "7" in the score, Carole Finer chose to sing seven folk songs with a banjo. Feldman stood up and shouted it down on the grounds that this was "not the music of Christian Wolff."[12]

A few days later, Wolff told an interviewer from Belgrade Television that he was "at a "transitional point." He had learned how "to write music which is available for a number of performers, which allows the performers to actively take part in the music, be responsible for the music, but which does not abandon them." The new question for him was how to combine his political concerns with his music. "I cannot find a solution to the social problems right now. I would like to learn much more about them [and] I would like to relate my music to them as much as possible."[13]

The intellectual path to that wish was subtle but perhaps inevitable. Wolff's parents and many in the Washington Square community in which Wolff grew up leaned toward the Left, though as a boy Christian knew little more of politics from them than that Democrats were preferable to Republicans. His parents were antifascist, of course, but a few of their friends sympathized with the U.S. brand of Communism that the McCarthy hearings endeavored to uproot. "Bolshevism" had held up ideals that attracted many people who were born in and raised during the Depression. Americans had even fought on the same side as Russia in World War II. But as the failures of Stalinism (and Stalin himself) became known and the Cold War began to set in, U.S. Communism had to retrench.

Wolff had declared himself a pacifist in 1959. In the early 1960s, Wolff had sometimes taught as a volunteer in Harlem. In the mid-1960s, as both the Soviet Union and the United States dug in their heels, Mao and the People's Republic of China became the new models for those drawn to leftist ideals. As a university professor, even at conservative Harvard, Wolff encountered student rhetoric against the Vietnam War and in favor of equality for women and African Americans. In academia, radical politics was turning into a small but noisy orthodoxy. In music, protest and cultural critique abounded in folk and rock. Even in classical music, so mainstream a modernist composer as Luciano Berio had begun to question the social usefulness of this highly cultivated art form: in his bestselling 1969 Columbia LP of *Sinfonia*, one heard a speaker in the third movement passionately declare, "all this can't stop the wars . . . can't lower the price of bread."

Just after his residency at Darmstadt, Wolff got a commission from Rzewski for a new piano piece. Inspired by the one-man virtuosity and additive declamations of political text in Rzewski's own pieces *Coming Together* and *Attica*, Wolff's new work, *Accompaniments*, attempted to break from the "overly introverted feeling in much of my earlier music" and communicate more directly with an uninitiated audience.[14] Of the work's four sections, the second, third, and fourth were instrumental only. In the second and third, the pianist played fully notated angular melodies interspersed with rhythmic lines played on bass drum and high-hat cymbal—a nod to ceremonial Chinese music. In the fourth the pianist discarded the percussion instruments for a long contrapuntal piano solo.

Only the first section contained text. For that Wolff took a passage in praise of the Cultural Revolution from the Pantheon Books edition of Jan Myrdal and Gun Kessle's *China: The Revolution Continued.*[15] He divided that passage into units of one to sixteen syllables each (sometimes dividing words). For each unit of text Wolff made a series of sixteen four-note chords, all subsets of a larger fixed-pitch chord. With only a few constraints on how to coordinate between voice and piano, the performer would sing or chant each unit of text syllabically, accompanied by the designated chords for that unit. This resulted in a ritualized declamation of narrative propaganda over a carefully structured but highly flexible scaffolding, with each group of chords faintly echoing the restricted-pitch harmonies of his earliest music. Still, the sonorities were less the point for Wolff than were the discipline and "special alertness" that came with realizing the piece. In this case, the serious commitment needed to play *Accompaniments* matched the austerity of the text. Yet the virtuosity one needed undercut any pretense of proletarianism. This was music for a professional musician.

Wolff's musical "transitional point" came not so much in *Burdocks* or political intent, but in a new approach to melody that began with a series of piano pieces he wrote in 1969–70. Wolff had become acquainted with the work of U.S. composers Terry Riley, Steve Reich, and Philip Glass. Their so-called minimalist compositions transgressed common modernist rhetoric that relied on aperiodic rhythms, angular disjunct melodies and rapidly mutating harmony, usually hyperchromatic and filled with constant variation and rapid rates of change—in other words, all things one found in Wolff's music to that point. The minimalists instead favored pulse-oriented rhythms, pandiatonic harmony, incessant repetitions of short ideas, and a very slow rate of harmonic change. The sonic result lacked modernist mystery, preferring directness, approachability, and instant comprehension. If modernism had embraced introversion, the new style was extroverted, holding no secrets from its listeners, whom it invited to let the static sonorities and kaleidoscopic counterpoint wash over them. Slow, subtle changes now constituted musical rhetoric.

Wolff began writing a series of responses to minimalism, pieces in which he focused on melody—not in the abstract sense in which he had once said that all sounds end up, but in the more conventional sense: strings of pitches conceived as lines flowing through time. In this new transitional style, Wolff began with a set of pieces titled *Tilbury*, after his and Cardew's pianist friend John. In *Tilbury 1* (1969), Wolff returned for the first time in fifteen years to continuous staves across the page with noteheads and rests on a single staff (treble or any other clef, consistently maintained). The pitches cycled and permutated the same fourteen pitches within the range of E3 to F4. In this sense the piece could be seen as an extrapolation of his earliest pieces, but with a freedom of notation they had not used. There were only implicit rhythmic specifications (other than the rests) and the tempo could be modified ad lib. Embellishments and transpositions were welcome. Optional notes appeared in parentheses. The dynamic was generally soft.

The sequel, *Tilbury 2 & 3* had a similar score format to *Tilbury 1*, but its notation was divisible into two different realizations: "2" was for solo instrument, and "3" was for multiple instruments. Unlike *Tilbury 1* this score specified rhythmic values (though not the coordination among parts), the range was enormous, with the lines now very disjunct. It was to *Tilbury 1* what, almost twenty years earlier, *For Piano II* had been to *For Piano I.*

If the *Tilbury* pieces were inspired by minimalism, as Wolff suggests, they diverged from that style in several ways: they were not pulse-oriented; the clefs were indeterminate; they were not diatonic; and they called for free ornamentation. A more persuasive homage to minimalism came in the early 1970 piece *Snowdrop*, the first commissioned work Wolff had written in ten years. Scored for harpsichord "and (or) possibly other instruments," the piece consisted mostly of runs of single- or double-beamed notes (without clefs) in various configurations that were interrupted by frequent pauses. The patterning of these runs seemed as systematic and comprehensive as some of his earliest pieces:

— one voice running up or down either conjunctly, disjunctly, or both
— two voices running up or down—overlapping by various amounts and either in contrary or similar motion to the other—with either both conjunct, both disjunct, one conjunct the other disjunct, or mixtures of both

Most of the piece was chromatic, but progressed to a very long white-key passage that was the first time Wolff had used overtly diatonic harmony.

In these keyboard pieces, what traditionally would have been considered a sketch or precompositional catalog of materials now became the score. In other words, as in much of Feldman's and Brown's music, the composer laid out the most typical "traditional" aspects of the score, but let performers work out the details. When compared to most of Wolff's scores of the 1960s, with more open scoring but complex rules, the simple layout of the *Tilbury* pieces and *Snowdrop* seemed relatively conventional, designed to encourage performance without too many particular constraints. Perhaps not surprisingly, critics took to these simpler works. Donal Henahan of the *New York Times* could hear the *Tilbury* pieces "beckoning the listener inside [their] attenuated sounds to hear their essence."[16] Brian Dennis, writing for the *Musical Times*, said that *Snowdrop* was "an intriguing interplay of scale fragments drifting together and then apart in random arabesques."[17]

Wolff further refined and regularized his new interest in melody via the *Exercises*, a personal genre he would pursue for years to come. It began as a set of fourteen concise works written during 1973–74 (with occasional additions in later years). These pieces were for an open ensemble that would form a microcosmic society in which players worked together yet responded to one another heterophonously, all players attempting to play in unison with one another, yet inevitably spilling over others' attacks and releases. Although in some ways these exercises mimicked the loose-weaved texture of Old South congregational singing (and the Ba-Benzélé music Wolff admired), they prompted Cage to say they sounded like "classical music of an unknown civilization."[18]

Though each exercise had its own particulars, the predominant score layout was a single long string of open or filled noteheads (with or without stems or beams) to be played in the clef or clefs of the instruments involved, with occasional pauses (represented by small wedges). The players would collectively adopt a consistent flow of notes, with individual variations allowed, so long as unison playing was, according to the performance notes, "the point of reference" to which a player should return. If the score gave a midground between reading and improvisation, the making of it was a midground between planning and improvisation: "to write with an at once free and focused immediacy analogous to a kind of instrumental improvisation, the written result of which would in turn allow the performers to play in that same spirit." Wolff's guiding principle was now this: "Let playing be composition and composition playing."[19]

The exercises distilled Wolff's recent concerns. They embodied simplicity and flexibility. They also had the educative conceit suggested by the title: one was learning how to behave among different musical personalities, but free from the normal dictates of "chamber music." For these reasons, the exercises continue to be among the most performed repertoire of Wolff's career, in venues ranging from concert halls to clubs to classrooms.

Just when Wolff had begun composing the exercises, Feldman finally organized an event about which he and Cage had been talking for years: the first concert devoted entirely to Wolff's music. To understand its importance, one must consider the internal dynamics of the increasingly well-known New York School. In 1952 Cage had welcomed Earle Brown to collaborate in various ways

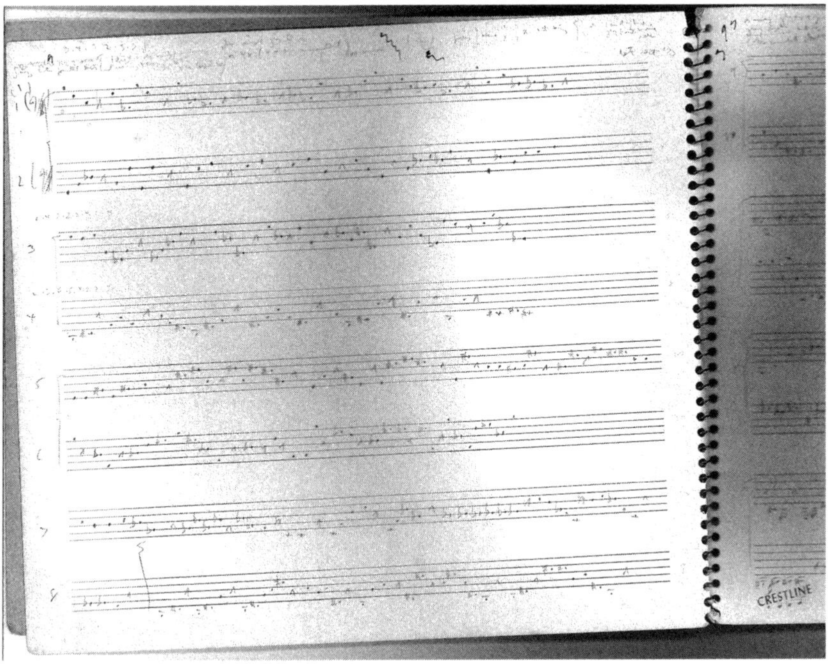

Figure 7. The sketch page for the first of Wolff's exercises—virtually indistinguishable from the "finished" score. Wolff Papers. Used by permission.

with himself, Wolff, Feldman, and Tudor. Feldman, however, "refused [Brown] admittance" into their circle. Feldman "became very, very angry," Cage said, and so, "my friendship with Morty was broken for quite a period."[20] Wolff himself tried to intervene and reconcile Cage and Feldman.[21]

To help repair the rift, Cage mounted a joint concert of Brown's and Feldman's work on 11 October 1963 in Town Hall. The short-term benefit of this concert was to salve their feelings. But the long-term detriment, Cage later explained, "was that no concert was ever given of the work of Christian Wolff. And his work, as a result, is not noticed as much as Earle and Morty's."[22] In the mid-1960s, Feldman and Cage had spoken often about remediating Wolff's neglect by giving him his own concert. In March 1970, Cage assessed a Whitney Museum concert of New York School music in this way: "I found the entire evening nearly unbearable; [it] bored me so deeply"—except, he said for "my still very keen interest in Christian Wolff's music."[23] Meanwhile, Feldman, when talking about the New York School, often referred only to himself, Cage, and Wolff, leaving out Brown. On one occasion in the 1960s, Feldman was asked how the New York School members lined up with those of the Second Viennese School. Cage was Schoenberg, Feldman said, he himself was Berg, and Wolff was Webern. Someone asked, what about Brown? Krenek, Feldman replied.[24]

Now, having joined the faculty at SUNY Buffalo, Feldman was able to mount the long-discussed Wolff concert there on 15 April 1973. It included what Feldman called "the masterwork of that period [the early 1950s]," *Nine*, which, though it had been played once before (Prague, 1962), Wolff still had never heard. "Just imagine," Feldman said, "here was a composer who astonished the New York avant-garde at sixteen or seventeen."[25] Feldman recounted to the audience Cage's first encounter with Wolff, explained that Wolff's importance was now "equal to Webern's," called Wolff's music Cage's "North Star," and added that "I think of [Wolff] as my artistic conscience."[26]

5 Something More Specifically "Musical": 1973–1984

AT DARTMOUTH, WOLFF CONSTANTLY had to prepare new lesson plans. Throughout the 1970s, he manned three to five courses a year in comparative literature, humanities, classics in Greek and Latin (as well as in translation), Greek tragedy, Homeric poetry, Marxist literature, and special-topics courses that explored subjects such as Eros, political philosophy, and feminism. During his first year at Dartmouth (1970–71), Wolff also started a "Workshop in Experimental Music," loosely based on his workshops in British art schools. He enrolled workshop members not by audition but by interviews in which students, regardless of their musical training, had to commit to collaborate with one another in assorted sonic behaviors. Each workshop varied in enrollment (usually from twelve to twenty-five) and had students ranging from musically skilled, ambitious young instrumentalists to theater and art students. The workshop's repertoire featured open scores—Wolff's own pieces, some Cage, some Oliveros, some Rzewski, et al.—and even the students' own new works. They also played arrangements of folk tunes and even classical pieces (e.g., piano preludes of Chopin) for whatever instruments and voices were available. Halfway through the course, the class collectively decided what they liked to play, assessed what "worked," and planned a concert (preferably off campus), collaborating on location, program, poster design, transportation, and so forth.

Early in 1973 Wolff gave a lecture to the Dartmouth faculty in which he brought together his divided assignments.[1] The lecture, "Plato and the New Music," was formal and cool-headed but polemical. Wolff explained Plato's belief in music's power to shape character and transform the soul in ways a good society requires. Citing passages from the *Phaedo*, the *Statesman*, the *Republic*, and the *Laws*, Wolff traced Plato's critique of the "new" music that debased a society by freeing melody from the support of words, misusing the modes, or needlessly complicating rhythms. He then pivoted to Mao's Yenan talks, in which he saw the modern continuation of Plato's critique, and praised the Cultural Revolution (though its brutal practices were not yet known in the West). With Plato and Mao as a foundation, Wolff explicitly echoed Cardew in indicting avant-garde composers—Elliott Carter, to name one—for their elitism and self-absorbed styles.

Nevertheless, Wolff and Cardew's outlooks grew increasingly distinct. When on 20 May 1973 Cardew mounted a performance of Wolff's *Accompaniments* (alongside Rzewski's *Attica* and *Coming Together*), Cardew rose to attack not Wolff's music, he said, but Wolff's choice of subjects: pollution and the population explosion, two of the causes that had emerged in the U.S. counterculture in the late 1960s alongside civil rights, women's rights, economic justice, and resistance to the Vietnam War. Cardew considered environmentalism and birth control the "great red herrings" of the U.S. intellectual elite. Now Wolff had shown himself "an erring brother" duped by the pseudocollectivism of the academic bourgeois. He and Rzewski had created "confusion" by their elitism dressed up as proletarianism. The point of his offering this Wolff-Rzewski concert, Cardew said, was "to bring these ideological and political lines out into the open and take a conscious stand against them and criticize them."[2]

Cardew wanted to court the proletarian masses on a grand scale. Wolff wanted to create a commemorative, nondogmatic body of personal narratives of workers' struggles for justice. John Tilbury—friend of both composers—saw another distinction: Cardew "sacrificed all on the altar of revolution." But Wolff's works, even the earlier ones, he found to be already "a projection into the future, a utopian paradigm; they *are* political. The music-making they generate is collaborative, self-consciously giving and taking, non-judgmental, respectful, attentive, sharing, cherishing the quotidian, where *individuality*, not 'individualism,' is nurtured. In short, it is strongly anti-authoritarian, 'democratic.'"[3] From Wolff's perspective, Cardew had "a kind of proselyting streak," whereas "the aim [for me] is not to say 'This is what you must think,' but to get people to look at things and think about them." If Cardew was an evangelist, Wolff was—not surprisingly—a professor.

In that he followed Cage's teacherly example. Yet Wolff continued to spar gently with Cage about overtly political music. In January 1974 Cage wrote to Wolff to question the emphasis Wolff now placed on the idea of "power" in his music. Cage began, in effect, by revising his own history, saying how he would have stopped writing music altogether in the 1940s were it not for the rejuvenating message of Asian thought, which could be summarized as: stop trying to control. Even though Cage's faith in that dictum is arguable, he claimed now to take delight in "not exercising power over sounds." But he had come to the conclusion that such an approach to music could not change society. He had to ask, "What is right action for musicians to bring about the revolution?"[4]

Two months later, Wolff replied with a brief letter that heartily quoted Ives: "The future of music may not lie entirely with music itself but rather in the way it encourages and extends, rather than limits, the aspirations and ideals of the people," etc. Attached to this letter were miscellaneous notes and musings by Wolff on the subject of music and politics, along with his notes to "Plato and the New Music," which he had now delivered in various mutations twice more (at UC Santa Cruz and Smith College).[5]

That summer, Wolff was invited back to Darmstadt. During the last full week of July 1974, he held class there each weekday afternoon for an hour, treating the social concerns of music and introducing the latest music of American composers in his immediate circle (as well as, notably, Philip Glass). The Darmstadt students questioned the intent, durability, and permanence of much of this music, simpleminded as it seemed by Darmstadt's usual standards: beat-driven, redundant, modal, and conventionally "melodic." Even the texts of some of the music—especially Rzewski's *Attica*—struck Darmstadt hearers as too blatant, too vernacular. Wolff's replies to his critics, however, seemed less important than the mere fact of their location: he had carved out a place for minimalists and political music in the heart of serial orthodoxy. How one might measure the success of the move is difficult to say. But he was not invited back for twenty-four years.

Wolff increasingly relied on "pick-up groups" of friends for premiers. He had always had a core of composer-performer friends (Tudor, Rzewski, Behrman, Cardew, Cage, et al.) as well as a few virtuoso instrumentalists who admired and played his work (trombonist Garrett List, for example, or French horn player Kurt Schwertsik). To frequently premiere new works with regular cohorts actually became in his mind a part of "socially conscious" music: the bonding of a small collective of mutually reliant players embodied the cooperative political life he imagined through his texts and techniques.

But beyond the social consciousness of his performance collective, Wolff turned to a new technique: the veiled embedding of old worker's songs and political tunes in the fabric of his counterpoint. "Veiled" in that he transformed the tunes largely by techniques we discuss below.[6] This constituted a kind of cryptography that harked back to the Middle Ages, privileging the associative power of tunes tied to specific words. It was an esoteric act of devotion to an idea, one presuming an initiated and sympathetic body of hearers. Wolff's new music derived from old worker songs was an allusive homage to the struggles of the Industrial Age, in which the original materials were, in effect, melted down and recast. To make the homage clear, though, Wolff often presented the songs directly at the pieces' openings (e.g., *Bread and Roses*, *Death of Mother Jones*, and *Cello Variations on "Hallelujah, I'm a Bum"*) or encouraged the players to play the songs in their original form before playing the new, derived pieces.

He drew his tunes mainly from three sources. One was a 1973 Dover Books reissue of the 1960 anthology by Edith Fowke and Joe Glazer: *Songs of Work and Protest*, which included many militant and humorous songs. Another was Pete Seeger's hefty autobiography-songbook *The Incompleat Folksinger*, which Simon and Schuster had published in 1972. The third was John Lomax and Alan Lomax's venerable *Folk Song U.S.A.*, first published in 1947 with the musical editorship of Charles Seeger and his wife, Ruth Crawford Seeger.[7]

With only a few exceptions—mainly new folk songs, such as Holly Near's "Hay Una Mujer Desaparecida"—Wolff drew from such anthologies the songs that would permeate his music for the remainder of his career: During the 1970s–80s alone, he used as source material these political and folk songs found in the aforementioned three books alone (listed here in the order he used them):

There Once Was a Union Maid
Hallelujah, I'm a Bum
Bread and Roses
John Golden and The Lawrence Strike
The Preacher and the Slave
Moorsoldaten (Peat-Bog Soldier)
Rock About
Abi Yoyo
Po' Lazarus
Big Rock Candy Mountain
Acres of Clams
Hey Ho, Nobody Home
The Sun Is Burning

Mary, Don't You Weep
O Freedom
Set Down, Servant
Ain't No More Cane in Dis Brazis
Joshua Fit the Battle of Jericho
The Grey Goose
All the Pretty Little Horses
Cindy

His earliest and most overt use of one of these songs led to an almost legendary moment in experimentalist lore, one that drove a temporary wedge in his relationship with Cage. Since 1964, Merce Cunningham had staged what he called simply "events." An "event" was a performance by his dance troupe in which old choreographies were spliced together into medleys underlaid with fresh music. In the fall of 1975, Cunningham commissioned Wolff for some new music for his next event. Wolff responded with four new exercises (nos. 15–18). The first two exercises of this new set—one for piano, the other for unspecified duet—derived their material from *Union Maid.* The fourth (open instrumentation quartet) derived from *Hallelujah, I'm a Bum.* Cunningham used these new exercises to accompany one of the events Cunningham held during the first week of December. Before playing the Exercises, Wolff's players raucously sang *Union Maid* itself "because we were in sympathy with its sentiments." Wolff recalls: "The audience, most of whom routinely had encountered and tolerated the most advanced kinds of music, audibly gasped in shock." While a few audience members (and even dancers) spoke well of it, most dismissed it. Even Holly thought it beyond the pale and told Christian so. Cage turned away from Wolff, visibly disturbed.[8]

Two weeks later, Wolff wrote Cage to apologize for the "troublesome diversion" he and his group had caused. He explained that it was a "fair risk," given the witty, even comic, choreographic tone (and juxtapositions) Cunningham often used. But part of the problem, Wolff explained, was that Cage claimed to have renounced "intentions" and Wolff could not do the same. "Perhaps I should let go of the sounds; I can't seem to let the intentions go. But I seem now to be determined to continue to try to bring them together. I don't know what else to do."[9]

Earlier that year Neely Bruce commissioned Wolff to write his first choral piece. Bruce was one of a small but active group of American composer-performer-scholars (many of them former students of Charles Hamm at the University of Illinois) who studied twentieth-century American vernacular music, composed music that abstrusely referenced its idioms, and performed both vernacular and experimental music. (Bruce and the similarly Americana-minded William Brooks, for example, both played in Cage's *HPSCHD* at Illinois in 1969.) In a sense, they continued a line begun by the Charles and Ruth Crawford Seeger (whose children and stepchildren included Pete, Peggy, and Mike Seeger, all icons of the folk revival). Now teaching at Wesleyan—the university that had published all of Cage's books—Bruce wanted Wolff to write a new work for his student and community chorus.

For source material, Wolff turned to two principal sources. One was the autobiography of Bill Haywood, leader of the so-called Wobblies—members of the IWW union (Industrial Workers of the World)—a group well-known for its ideological straddling of socialism and anarchism. The other source was *Songs of Work and Protest*, which contained many of the Wobblies' militant and comic songs. With these as textual foundations, Wolff wrote a strongly didactic multi-movement work for chorus, keyboard, and two unspecified solo-line instruments, using mostly simple melodies and deployment of text, favoring unison syllabic declamations and vocal hocketing,

The piece, simply titled *Wobbly Music*, began with a kind of exposition via the straightforward singing of three workers songs: "Bread and Roses," "John Golden and the Lawrence Strike," and "The Preacher and the Slave" (aka "Pie in the Sky"). A choralelike instrumental interlude prepared the listener for the four movements to follow. The first of these set to music portions of the 1908 preamble to the constitution of the IWW, using hocketed voices occasionally interrupted by bass figurations. The second movement loosely arranged "John Golden" with "unison" (i.e., heterophonic) singing over ad lib. accompaniment. The third took a text from Arturo Giovannitti's closing statement at the Lawrence Strike trial in 1912 and set it with chanting, recitatives, and chordal accompaniment. The fourth used a text from a Bill Haywood speech (1913), setting it with a narrow, Exerciselike tune in vocal hocket with occasional instrumental doublings and percussion-chord interjections (à la *Accompaniments*). The whole set seemed to convert early twentieth-century strikers' rhetoric into a kind of liturgy fit for declamatory, ritualized delivery. Wolff would later call it "my most successful piece in that line."[10] Rzewski was more definitive: "I consider [it] a masterpiece of modern choral literature."[11]

Wobbly Music crossed several thresholds for the composer. It was his first choral work (and indeed one of his few vocal pieces at all). It put forth for the first time what would become his canon of musico-political sources: the worker's music championed by folk revivalists of the 1950s and 1960s. It exploited a technique that had long fascinated him: hocket, the medieval practice of dividing a single line among different players (a technique Webern too had used in his celebrated orchestration of the Ricercare from J. S. Bach's *Musical Offering*). Here the political usefulness of vocal hocketing became clear. Wolff could present a text prismatically by refracting its components (words or pairs of words) in various vocal parts. That kept the text semantically intact but shifted its colors and spatial placement (i.e., from one group's position on the stage to another's). Modernist composers (e.g., Berio) and experimentalist composers (e.g., Kenneth Gaburo) had tended to treat texts as phonemic objects ready to be dismantled and recombined, often in thick nets of counterpoint. Wolff's monophonic-heterophonic hocketing in *Wobbly Music* allowed him to present the text with no obscuring of meaning, yet still musically "developed."

As Wolff began to receive more commissions, his old methods had to give way. In the 1960s he had intended new works to be played and playable by untrained performers—or rather, performers whose training required only the skills needed for his idiosyncratic scores. In that way—true to a certain democratic politics—conventional virtuosi had little if any advantage over beginners in performing a Wolff composition. But from the mid-1970s on, old styles of notation and technique took fresh root in Wolff's writing. As he explained in 1980, in pieces such as *Burdocks* "there is a sense in the background of nature and of people (including children) playing." But in the later works "there is something more specifically 'musical' and a kind of expression that is more evidently musical—that is, closer to historical continuities" of what has been called "music."[12] He now believed that "music can function better socially if it is more clearly identified with what most people recognize as music."[13]

Some of the changes in the *way* he wrote grew from changes in his household. In fall 1975 Holly got a room near Harvard so she could retreat several days a week to work on her doctoral dissertation, a comparative study of narrative structure in three epic poems (*Gilgamesh*, the *Odyssey*, and *Beowulf*). As his academic and parental duties expanded, Wolff's method turned more and more piecemeal. He likened it to "journal entries" or, more commonly, "quilting."[14] By the former, he meant short, occasional notations of pitch, rhythm, form, and so forth, usually one concise page (or portion of a page) at a sitting. By "quilting," he meant how he would browse through the "journal entry" pages, pick those that seemed to work well together—however juxtapositionally—and assemble them into larger forms. "I think of Cage's notion of 'sounds for themselves,'" he later wrote, "each sound its own center, then always possible interpenetrations; but instead of just the single sound or sound event, I also, and mostly, use various longer continuities of sounds. This is not unrelated to, say, Satie or Stravinsky (or Frescobaldi)."[15]

His music courses also seemed to use a similar "quilting" technique. Consider the Music 3 course he taught with Malcolm Goldstein in the winter term of 1977. The course began with reviews of rhythm, melody, acoustics, and perception. It proceeded to electronic music, followed by "form and continuity," Beethoven, African American music, Japanese music, Renaissance music, and finally "political and popular music." The students not only read from an eclectic library of titles (including Cage's *Silence*, Charles Keil's *Urban Blues*, Leonard Meyer's *Emotion and Meaning in Music*, and Cardew's *Stockhausen Serves Imperialism*, to name a few) but also wrote and performed two new compositions apiece.

One can scarcely reconstruct the methods Wolff used to compose any individual piece from this era (and beyond). Even Wolff himself seldom recalls. Few "sketches" or drafts exist. Although he tended to be systematic within limited frameworks, he stayed open to breaching his methods at will. Momentary instinct could always override a system. Most pieces were sewn together from fragments. As for the fragments themselves, to shift the metaphor, Wolff's construction of them resembled glassblowing: the glassblower either blows a usable shape or discards the flawed results. As Wolff wrote each prospective portion of a piece he considered it, then either kept it or threw it away.

Two constants in the music of this period are the terseness of his gestures, a trait that pervades his music from its earliest to latest incarnations, and through-composed forms, which he felt necessary to embody progression, a constant moving forward, never back. At the same time, no one compositional *method* characterizes Wolff's political music. Not only did each piece constitute a quilt of fragments, but the pieces taken together made up a larger patchwork of compositions. Because Wolff resisted the exact repetition of compositional methods from piece to piece, his style constantly, though subtly, realigned itself.

Although unwilling to fully submit sounds to predetermined plans, Wolff still harnessed instinct with numeric controls and, sometimes, archaic contrapuntal procedures. That latter phrase alludes in part to his treatment of pitch as series of "points," individual tones that he often took from the first few notes of a folk tune by systematic transpositions. He principally used two methods to do so:

1. Quasi-serial metamorphosis of a folk incipit: This consisted of applying the same interval of transposition—either up or down—to each note of the first few notes of a folk tune. This could take place in many layers. He might transpose each note up or down a half step, then the resultant tune's pitches up or down another half step, etc., gradually transforming the original fragment by slim degrees. Or he might transpose each note up or down either of two intervals—a half step or a major third, for example—and then do the same to the resultant

melody, repeatedly. Or, again, he might transpose each note up or down a half step; then, on a second pass (either to the original tune or the resultant one) up or down a whole step; then, again, up or down a minor third; then a major third; and so forth, through all the intervals to a preset limit (generally a tritone); then, possibly, reverse direction (fourths to thirds, to seconds).

2. With or without the technique in no. 1, he might spontaneously change (or allow the player to change) the clef, permutating many of the tune's interval qualities (e.g., half and whole steps).

Beyond these pitch-only transformations, he used various manipulations of pitch + rhythm. One of these is a simple additive technique. In one version of it, Wolff unfolds a tune by playing its first note (i.e., pitch and rhythm combined), then the first and second (1 + 2), then (1 + 2 + 3), then (1 + 2 + 3 + 4), and so forth (similar to the entire performance process of Rzewski's 1969 *Les Moutons de Panurge*). Since such a process is so transparent, Wolff uses it sparingly. A more interesting and durable version of the technique involves separating the parameters: Wolff uses the pitches in their original order but unfolds the rhythmic values additively (and thus more slowly, while the pitches go on independently). Thus:

Original Pitches
1 2 3 4 5 6 etc.
Original Rhythms
1 1 2 1 2 3 etc.

A reverse of this procedure is, of course, also possible: the original rhythms appear in order, but the pitches additively.

Wolff could also adopt another, more elaborate technique that he calls loops on a grid: a quasi-isorhythmic technique illustrated via the example of figure 8.

In this example, Wolff begins with three pitches in the treble clef (A4, B4, D4) and three in the bass clef (C4, E3, F3). To the treble clef he assigns the number series [3.4.0.1.12]; to the bass [5.2.2.10.1]. He then marks off a series of thirty-six units—not beats or measures, per se, but simply spaces, or what we will, for the purposes of this description, call "slots," into which he will place each note. In the treble clef he starts by placing A4 in the first slot, skips three slots, places A4 in the next slot, skips four slots, places A4 in the next slot, then another in the next slot (i.e., has "0" slots intervening), skips 1 slot and places another A4, then 12 and places yet another, completing the series [3.4.0.1.12]. Next, he skips 3 from the last A4 and places a B4 in a slot, skips 4 and places another B4, followed by one more in the next slot (i.e., "0" slots intervening), which is the last slot of the 36. At this point he "loops" to the first slot, skips it (i.e., "1") and places another

Figure 8. A sample of Wolff's "loops-on-a-grid" sketch technique. Gift of Christian Wolff to authors.

B4, skips 12 and places another. He then skips 3 slots and places a D4, skips 4 and places another, and so forth. He follows the same process in the bass clef, using its respective pitches and number series. This produces a constant kaleidoscopic reconfiguring of the six pitches as solo notes or simultaneities. With that done he translates the reconfigurations into simple measures and rhythms. The result resembles the kind of work he did with limited pitch pieces in his earliest years, only now more systematic in procedure.

All these procedures can be mixed within the same passage, juxtaposed within the same piece, or abandoned at will. Strangely, they bespeak an ambivalence to the politically charged source material they transform: one can rarely recognize more than glimpses of the songs whose texts mean so much to the composer. The loops on a grid technique that Wolff developed hints that he has an implicit faith in their latent communicative power, but needs to refract them through a late-modern sensibility. Well-trained in translating archaic languages into English or tracing single themes across genres in literature, he now translated folk music into experimental music with this technique. By mapping one system onto another, he converted the common or demotic musical language into an arcane and hieratic one. But what mattered more than procedures were the results. In the latter half of the 1970s, one could see a refinement—even a kind of taming—of Wolff's musical rhetoric. To see that, consider two of the virtuosic piano pieces he composed during those years: *Bread and Roses* and *Hay Una Mujer Desaparecida*.

Both works grew from solo piano genres that both Cardew and Rzewski had embraced. Cardew wrote his neoromantic *Thälmann Variations* in 1975; Cage and others thought the piece "19th century salon music."[16] In the same year, Rzewski had written what for Wolff was the ideal composing-out of variations on one of South America's most beloved political chants or songs (equivalent in iconic power to the civil rights movement's "We Shall Overcome"). Rzewski's *The People United Shall Never Be Defeated* sprang from "grand manner" traditions quite at odds with the kind of virtuosity in Wolff's earlier piano works. The piece was populist in its appeal to historic pianism but progressive not only in its leftist allusions but in its huge variety of styles.

Wolff followed suit in the piano works he wrote in the late 1970s (often for Rzewski to play). Just as Rzewski's *Attica* and *Coming Together* had inspired Wolff to use textual declamations over simple accompaniment, *The People United* inspired him to write in long variation forms for solo piano with no text, only the musical foundation of political song. And now, whereas his early solo piano works had been atomistic, these new ones were aphoristic. They relied not on modular points or moments but on strong, terse gestures strung into an abstract narrative. His earlier conventionally notated solo piano works had been shaped neither by dynamics nor articulations. They embodied a strictly Apollonian constructivist spirit, teetering on the precipice of unplayability. In their pianistic oratory his new works seemed far more Dionysian. And the variation genre seemed an apt vessel for his new style: it fit perfectly with his idea of quilting but gave a controlling formal concept.

Wolff wrote *Bread and Roses* (piano version) for Rzewski in 1976. In the notation, as with most of Wolff's pieces from then on, there is little on which to remark. He clearly determines pitches and rhythms, except for rests, which appear only as breath marks. The work consists of a variety of textures, which, according to the program note, are "freely stitched together":

huge, multiregistral chordal fanfares (most of them technically unplayable as actual simultaneities)
the tune, simply stated and harmonized
solo compound melodic lines in sixteenth notes
a treble-only, quarter note oriented solo-line variation
two-voice running sixteenth notes in counterpoint
solo-line fragments

The piece relies on long-breathed lines, either solo or in two-part counterpoint. These often amount to unidirectional arpeggiations that, as they spiral off, yield to twice- and thrice-repeated notes that seem to provide points of polarity. The long strings of equal note values (usually sixteenth notes) conjure faint echoes of the Baroque. But although the notes are generally written in (unmetered) conventional notation, the tempo, dynamics, and "ways of playing" are, in Wolff's words, "free and variable." This creates a densely thicketed rhapsody that, in Rzewski's words, listeners "seem to begin to enjoy only after they've heard it a couple of times."[17]

By contrast, *Hay Una Mujer Desaparecida* (1979) seemed domesticated, its textures combed out. With the same conventional notation as *Bread and Roses,* it provided a lean, more accessible set of character variations that were in many ways classicistic, with a much slower turnover of the total chromatic. The lines were now constrained, far from the ferocious disjunctures of interval and register in *Bread and Roses.* It even used barlines, though at irregular distances, to establish partitions between successive textures and rhythmic patterning. Throughout, it hinted at the populist vocabulary of other leftist composers from Copland to Cardew.

Between Wolff's writing of these two pieces—amid many other instrumental works—the ever-entrepreneurial Cage made plans with Wesleyan in 1977 to publish his earlier political correspondence with Wolff in his next book, *Empty Words.* Wolff fleshed out his earlier notes and drafted a new letter surveying his musico-political beliefs. He adopted a gentler tone, downplaying the possibility of music ever changing the world or solving its problems. Nevertheless, through collective action and revolutionary music, "I'd like to help, at least, to make myself and others less nervous at the prospect of real change"—including "dismantling capitalism."[18] In the end, Cage's editor cut the correspondence from the book. "I am both sorry and relieved," Cage wrote, "as I imagine you are too."[19] If there was a sequel to this proposed publication, it came in 1980 with Wolff's essay in the inaugural issue of Pozzi Escot and Robert Cogan's journal, *Sonus: A Journal of Investigations into Global Musical Possibilities.* Titled "On Political Texts and New Music," it continued what had begun as "Plato and the New Music." Wolff surveyed the political connotations of his earlier open-score untexted works, then gave detailed descriptions of his texted *Accompaniments* and *Wobbly Music.* These were, in effect, the new pillars in his post-Cardew opus.

Wolff wrote that essay amid new events in his family and career. In 1978 Holly finished her dissertation and got her doctorate in comparative literature. In 1979, she gave birth to their third child, Nicholas ("Tico"), and, in 1981, their fourth, Tristram. In 1978 Christian had finally been granted tenure at Dartmouth—far later than he had expected. Although he taught courses in language and literature,

Wolff's dual career had tilted almost entirely toward music. All through the 1970s he had obtained residencies at music schools, lectured on his own compositions, and attended concerts of new works—or even concerts devoted entirely to his music in London, West Berlin, Milan, and Budapest. In his 1981 *Modern Music*, Paul Griffiths discussed "The Cage Group," devoting one score excerpt apiece to Wolff, Feldman, and Brown (in that order) and lucidly explaining Wolff's pioneering scores. Interviews with Wolff and articles about his music appeared in Europe and the United States. Recordings came out on many labels, including Wergo, Vox, Electrola, EMI, and CRI. But throughout the entire decade he had only three academic paper readings and two journal articles in classics (1973 and 1979).

Still, Wolff pursued opportunities and responded to invitations related to his avowed scholarly passion. Having developed a wide circle of friends in the field (some former students who had gone on to positions in classics at various universities), he could give public addresses on Euripides' and Sophocles' plays during 1980 and a few years thereafter at conferences and guest lectureships at Smith, Brown, Princeton, and Oxford. He even took a brief stint as a visiting professor in the Harvard Classics Department.

In 1984 Wolff turned fifty. It is tempting to call what Wolff had already been writing for the previous decade as some form of "late style," in which his scholarly aptitude for antiquity drove a technique that, at least on its surface, harked back to venerable traditions of expression and flow, despite its unbridled chromaticism. His music certainly had retrenched from his most radical experiments, those scores for which he was (and is) best known. One cannot well predict what shifts in style might yet come. "Late style" always depends on longevity. Still, as he passed through his hyperpolitical stage, Wolff renegotiated the radicalism of his music from its open-ended scoring to an ad hoc traditionalism. It was as though, in denying the ultrapopulism of Cardew, he turned to a style that honored the discipline and polish of performers who, more with each passing year, asked that he write for them. For the rest of the twentieth century, that style branched out in a genealogy of personal genres and titles, some of them attached to a medium that had long eluded him: the symphony orchestra.

6 Not to Do Something I've Already Done: 1982–1999

IN NOVEMBER 1982 JOHN CAGE turned seventy. By then, books and articles generally labeled Wolff as Cage's disciple, with little reciprocal influence implied. In a Cage birthday tribute Wolff wrote for *TriQuarterly*, he tried to adjust the historical lens. He conceded that Cage had hugely influenced him. After all, they had met when Wolff was an impressionable sixteen-year-old. Nevertheless, he said, Cage's real influence on him and others was his "discipline, uncompromisingness, asceticism, at the same time as his untiring declarations of support, cheerfulness, discovery and communication pleasure. His call for the use of intelligence and conscience." But no one could imitate Cage's music: "you would no more try to imitate it, if you had any sense, than you would try to duplicate a thunderstorm or the growing of grass."[1]

Just so, it would be difficult to imitate Wolff's music. Although it had mutated from its earliest and arguably most radical techniques, it followed a certain continuum. As we've noted, Cage described Wolff's exercises as "classical music of an unknown civilization."[2] In 1997, Dartmouth music chair Jon Appleton said that Wolff's music was "often unrelated to any known traditions."[3] The following year Rzewski described Wolff's music fulsomely: "Weird little tunes, sounding as if they had been beamed at some remote point in the universe and then bounced back again as a kind of intergalactic mutant music; recognizable melodic and rhythmic patterns, somehow sewn together in monstrous pairing, sometimes reminiscent of the demons of Hieronymous Bosch, composites of animals, fish, flowers, and common household objects: there is order, but also constant interruption, intrusions of disorderly reality upon regularity and lawfulness, combining to create an effect of both familiarity and strangeness. . . . not reproducing familiar forms, but revealing, behind these, life's unpredictability."[4]

By the year of Cage's seventieth birthday, Wolff had crossed the threshold into his (presumably) last style period, which encompassed a large body of pieces for diverse players, from solos (from flute to contrabass) to works for chamber groups of many sizes and combinations, though almost no "standard" ensembles.[5] What defined the style of this large body of works? Perhaps its most important—if seemingly superficial—trait is this: almost every score differs in its design and layout from every other. One finds in Wolff's late style a seemingly endless nonredundancy, an avid attempt to keep remixing notational styles and instructions. While he focuses intently on each segment of a piece when writing it, he keeps and revises only segments that please him or seem rich in possibility, then assembles those segments intuitively. "Stick it together and see what happens," he later said.[6] This is not mere fatalism. It appeals both to his earliest principles of embracing discontinuity and a desire to avoid formula. His ambition? "Not to do something I've already done."[7]

Cage had urged against waiting for ideas to percolate before going to work. Rather, he advocated working diligently and consistently. Wolff did the same, as much as possible amid his academic duties, familial obligations, and even farm chores (after Ray Nash passed away in 1982, Christian and Holly oversaw the farm and tended to mother Hope's needs). Compositional craft was fundamental, a kind of duty one owed to the raw material of sound. It also provided a kind of personal therapy for depressed moods: "Work is the only remedy I've found," he wrote to Rzewski, though it always had to be work that somehow felt "new."[8] Larry Polansky, a Dartmouth colleague of Wolff's since 1990, described what he observed about Wolff's writing process: "He has a small notebook that he carries, pretty much all the time—he must have hundreds of these things—and generally his compositional process is to simply write it, and then recopy it. His originals are done in pencil, and then he sits at his kitchen table and recopies. He's always writing, and he's very, very prolific, with a lot of little and big compositional systems that he uses so that, as a composer, he's remarkably free of compositional angst in a way. That is, he can keep writing pieces all the time without any kind of writer's block. Because he has evolved for himself so many systems that he can put to use and recombine in lots of ways and produce pieces."[9] Thus, looking back at the music of the 1980s–90s, Wolff had mostly hazy memories of their making: "I often don't remember how I made those pieces. I mean I look at [one and say]: 'Where the hell does this come from?' I wish I knew, because people ask me and I'm a little embarrassed to say that I just cannot remember."[10]

To analyze the resultant scores is difficult. They often contain no measure numbers or explicit time frames for parsing or comparison. They run the full notational spectrum from simple, unannotated common-practice notation (see *Bratislava*, 1995) to mostly coordination neumes (see *Digger Song*, 1988). Between those two poles one finds the majority of his scores: common-practice notation interleaved with mutations of Wolff's now "classic" new notations and instructions, though never in the same proportions or, indeed, with the same instructions or decisions delegated to performers. This was Wolff's new trope on atomistic construction, now manifest not within single pieces alone but across the span of his entire opus, each piece loosely disconnected from the others.

In these later works, one feels a new urgency. Wolff now seems more impatient with and even embarrassed by silence. Musical passages in which one might have expected gaps now get filled with notes. The music often doesn't breathe so much as gasp. Wolff no longer let sounds float but made it push forward. In his early works, he had associated silence with meditation, contemplation. But politics required activism. Political music couldn't weather the inertia that gaps of silence allowed. That musico-political activism continued in pieces not overtly political.

For a long time Wolff had privileged individual lines, not chords. In his later "notey" music, he tried to make those lines all "of a character that if they were to happen all by themselves, with absolutely nothing else going on, they would still have a good musical presence"—in other words, not just textural filler. By striving to maintain the quality of individual lines, Wolff felt that the emerging counterpoint would have the proper density and integrity. The lines that populate these later works tend to be long, twisting threads of pitches, with or without values attached, lines of varying lengths with little rhythmic pacing or design that connoted incept, development, or cadence. Sometimes the pitches are "all over" in register, but at other times notably constrained (as in the exercises) by the staff, a grid that attracts notes into its ambitus. These melodic lines most often consist of running sixteenth notes divided by wedge shapes for indeterminate pauses (the length of these could vary widely from player to player). The frequent coagulations of immediately repeated pitches (or pitch repetitions in close proximity) create small pockets of polarity, in which the listener seems to hear a "center" emerging—a center that quickly dissipates. This late music sometimes seems a species of sound design: no apparent underlying structural framework aside from atomism, à la Webern, yet highly ornamental.

Many solo pieces could convert to heterophonic ensemble pieces via written instructions, for example, "playable for one or more" of a given instrument; or with optional additional instruments allowed. As with the exercises (a personal genre to which he continued to add from the 1980s through the 1990s), the *unison* became the point of reference for each solo or ensemble piece: feel free to diverge slightly, but always return to synchronicity with the other player or players. By this time Wolff had worked with every sort of instrument and combination of instruments via his earlier open-instrumentation scores. Hearing and taking part in performances of those scores for many years had attuned him to instrumental techniques and idioms. Still, he continually returned to his own instrument, the piano.

On 16 September 1979, Rzewski had written a letter to Wolff congratulating him on the birth of his new son (though "I couldn't make out his name," Rzewski added, noting that Wolff's handwriting—a professorial scrawl—was "almost as illegible as my mother's.") More pressing was his request: "I'm badly in need of new piano pieces."[11] Rzewski, now a professor at the Royal Conservatory in Liège, regularly toured the continent playing his own and his friends' music, including Wolff's *Bread and Roses* and *Braverman Music*. After his September letter, Wolff sent Rzewski *Hay Una Mujer Desaparecida* and promised to write more piano music. In the meantime, Ursula Oppens (who had commissioned Rzewski's *The People United Will Never Be Defeated*) and Russian pianist Yvar Mikhashoff both asked Wolff for new pieces. This confluence of requests by virtuoso pianists led Wolff into a three-year period (1980–82) in which he wrote for almost nothing but piano.

All of these new works used Wolff's "notey" style and four of them—Exercises 19–20 (two pianos) and 21–22 (piano four hands)—heavily favored octave (or larger) simultaneities and two-note tremolandi that evoked nineteenth-century parlor music, though without its tonal moorings. Premiered by Oppens and Rzewski, Exercises 19 and 20 (subtitled "Harmonic Tremors" and "Acres of Clams") were written on a single grand staff for two pianos; Wolff instructs that players can distribute material between pianists at will, that is, dividing or doubling whatever they want. Nevertheless, Wolff gives very specific instructions on the division of labor and interactions in a piece, as in this paragraph from the performance notes in the score to Exercise 19:

> On pages 5 and 6, three sections of seven measures each are marked by double bars (after which, following the double bar with a fermata over it, there is the last section). After these three sections have been played, any one or more can be repeated. The players should agree

> before hand whether or not they will repeat and how many sections they will repeat (so that they can meet to play the last section); but, if repeating, each player decides independently which of two (if it was decided to repeat two) she or he will repeat or in what order (if it was decided to repeat three) (i.e. different parts of different sections may be combined); and whatever section a player may repeat he or she should only play one aspect of it, the melody line(s), the figurations, or the tremolos.[12]

Like virtually all of Wolff's pieces from this period, ones sense of musical progression derives largely from the evolution of activity and textures from beginning to end. Exercise 19, for example, begins with an almost chorale preludelike stratification of half notes in one line and, in the other, sixteenth notes grouped in nontriadic arpeggio groups of five, with occasional rests. By the end, the texture has mutated to an equally dense and active pair of lines increasingly laden with tremolos.

The most powerful (and probably durable) of his new piano music from these years was the set he wrote for Mikhashoff, a book of eleven preludes (1980–81), which the *American Record Guide* would call "quite simply among the most unusual and fascinating piano pieces of the second half of our century."[13] Almost every one of the preludes is a study in a particular texture, character, or pianistic technique. As is typical in this period of Wolff's music, they contain no tempo or dynamic indications (although he instructs that tempi can change at double bars, i.e., *within* preludes). All of the preludes are self-contained and have specific (overlapping) starting and ending dates of composition given as postscripts. A schematic of the set gives a nice précis of the kinds of techniques typically juxtaposed in Wolff's late style:

1. One or two lines on bass staff throughout, though with generous ledger lines (the highest note = D5); no barlines and mostly continuous sixteenth notes; empty spaces can be omitted, filled with silence, or filled with improvisation.

2. Intersecting loops of fragments that gradually disassemble; many dyads, though with increasing number of octave simultaneities; a wide range of rhythmic values, from thirty-second notes to half notes.

3. The full range of the piano explored with continuous very disjunct eighth notes until a double bar; thereafter, less disjunct continual sixteenths, punctuated by occasional eighth- or quarter-note rests.

4. Constant cross-cutting among types of behavior, including tempi (alternating between 80 and 120), sometimes as close as a bar apart; "x" noteheads used to indicate noises chosen by performers.

5. A repeatable one-system chorale of six- and seven-note chords in free

duration, with improvised whistled or hummed melody in unison rhythm with the chords.

6. Continual sixteenth-note runs (or eighth notes in the middle section), mostly one extreme register at a time, increasingly moving from single notes to dyads to two-part counterpoint to tremolos.

7. Mostly sixteenth notes (or sextuplets and septuplets) in two-voice counterpoint (lines occasionally in octaves), made sporadic by fermatas and other divisions interrupting the motion.

8. Rhythm stratified at the start: melody in long values in right hand with low eighths and sixteenths running in the left hand; after a double bar, the left hand slows down to quarters and halfs, then both hands take up mostly disjunct note-to-note counterpoint in eighths and some sixteenths. (The longest prelude of the set? cf. no. 10.)

9. Very short, with brief tremoloes almost constant in the right hand, the left hand mostly maintaining a constant eighth-note motion with many dyads and trichords for a rich lower texture.

10. Few accidentals throughout, mostly disjunct eighths (then some quarters) in an extremely disjunct three-voice counterpoint that must be carefully divided between hands; the last system a homorhythmic four-part chorale in eighths and quarters. (The longest of the set? cf. no. 8.)

11. Starts with a three- and four-voice chorale (based on the tune "Acres of Clams," which with new words had lately been used for the campaign against a nuclear power plant being built in Plymouth, New Hampshire); this appears in whole notes (whole note = 30–80; not clear whether each whole note can have a different duration or if a tempo in this range may be chosen for the passage); the chorale consists of a gradually shifting, enlarging, and contracting E♭ major pentatonic chord produced by the accumulating of the notes of the "Clams" tune; the rhythmic chronometry then accelerates into almost constant thirty-second notes, with longer notes (essentially the "Clams" tune with some octave shifts) occasionally resonating against them, long notes cued to appear each time the next note of the "Clams" tune appears.

His nonkeyboard solo works of this period—including works for flute, contrabass, electric guitar, snare drum, and koto—tended toward the jagged, halting lines one found in the piano pieces. At the same time, his duos, including many with piano, often had the give-and-take, shifting relationships of two-voice Baroque music, though with his hyperchromatic pitch vocabulary typically tied to epigrammatic series of equal-note values. Moreover, he continued what had now seemed necessary traits of his ensembles: in most situations involving multiple players, Wolff had either specific or optional contingencies for how players would relate to each other. These often involved some form of heterophony, the performers playing their parts as written but not attempting to align or synchronize beats or attack points.

In larger combinations, from trios to octets, mixed instrumental groups abound, standard combinations (e.g., string quartet, brass quintet) never appear, whether due to the commissioning artists or a continuing fascination with heterogeneity. Unusual trios appear (e.g., flute-percussion-cello, saxophone-electric guitar-double bass); quartets and larger groups typically feature one or two winds, one or two brass, one or two strings, sometimes piano, sometimes percussion. Meanwhile, from 1980 to 1999, there were only two works for open instrumentation: *Exercise X*, for seven or more players (1993), and his next work, *Or 4 People* (1994) for one to four players—and an expected duration of eight to thirty-five minutes.

Inspired by works of Iannis Xenakis, Wolff frequently used percussion in these late-century works, an instrumentation atypical of his earlier years. In retrospect, percussion had three obvious attractions. First, it was in a midground between fixed and open instrumentation: the type of *player* was determinate, but often could orchestrate at will (within loose parameters). Second, Wolff could bypass issues of pitch—always vexing in this late hour of Western harmonic vocabulary—and focus on rhythmic counterpoint. Third, percussion brought a sense of political militancy into his music. Although long given to the non-pulse-driven textures common in late modernism, he wanted now to turn to strong, decisive gestures and motives that characterized much music of the masses. Assertiveness, rather than passivity filled much of the political music he admired. Percussion helped infuse that trait into his new works.

A distinct personal genre Wolff developed in these years is what he calls the "peace march," whose name stems from a conventional form of antiwar protest in the 1960s–70s, in which the quasi-military act of marching became an antimilitary statement. This genre began with a solo flute piece (based on "Hey Ho Nobody Home") composed after he and family members had marched against the buildup of nuclear arms during 1983–84. This and later peace marches featured bold declamatory gestures, moving forward in a marchlike way with instruments—especially percussion—obliquely suggestive of military bands. Yet Wolff always varied the parameters of these pieces. Consider, for example, two of them written in succession: Peace March 2 (flute, clarinet, cello, piano, percussion) and Peace March 3 (flute, cello, percussion). The latter obviously employs a subset of the instruments in the former, but, typical of Wolff, subtly modifies the instructions, as seen in table 2.

Comparison of Score Specifications in Peace Marches 2 and 3

Peace March 2	Peace March 3
Tempo flexible within given range	Tempo free
Dynamics free (to be determined by players)	Dynamics given
Pitch specified	Pitches may be bent
Rhythm specified (though see below); sixteenth- and thirty-second notes dominate	Given rhythms may be "bent"; no values shorter than eight-notes (grace notes excepted)
Playable on its own	Should be played with another Peace March
Other: (1) If any part is too difficult, it may be modified (2) barlines may be construed as pauses	Other: (1) Play freely "as though getting out from under pressure" (2) Play "angry," i.e., "focusing anger, in order to make it useful"

A peace march could be a free-standing piece, a piece contingent on another piece, or, indeed. a movement of a larger work, as in the *Bowery Preludes* (1985–86). This set of five preludes was written for the Bowery Ensemble in New York: flute, trombone, percussion, piano. They typify Wolff's concerns and techniques from this period as he ostensibly connects to social causes but obscures with technique most of the connections. Preludes 1, 3, and 5 are based on songs (see below); the last of these preludes Wolff (in his program notes) called a peace march. Preludes 2 and 4, however, are not based on old songs but return to the open scoring of earlier pieces.

Each prelude differs in character and notation from the others. Prelude 1 unfolds in agitated block-chord fanfares alternating with contrapuntal duos that answer each other (flute-trombone against percussion-piano). Prelude 2 methodically coordinates two different synchronized pairs of instruments (flute-piano and trombone-percussion) in their rhythms, registers-timbres, and, unusually for Wolff, dynamics. Prelude 3, primarily a single line played heterophonically ad lib, is the most immediately disjunct and expansive in register, covering five octaves in its first three measures. Prelude 4 provides an interlude, a brief two-part invention for piccolo and trombone. The final prelude is essentially a quodlibet with added unpitched sounds and free lines embroidering the main tunes.

The songs from which he derives melodies in the *Bowery Preludes* link the piece to the civil rights movement. With one exception ("Picket Line Song"),

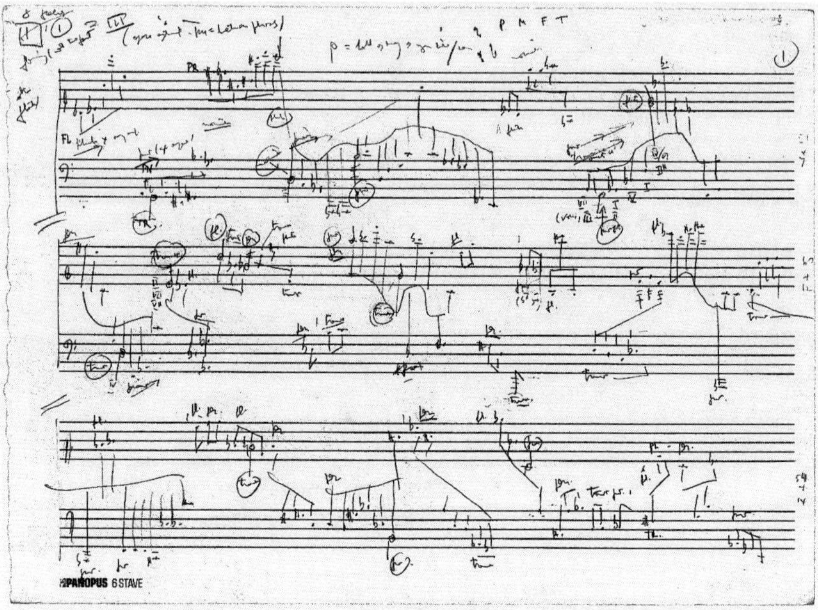

Figure 9. Sketch for the third of the *Bowery Preludes.* Wolff Papers. Used by permission.

they have African American origins or allusions: "Mary, Don't You Weep," "O Freedom," "Set Down, Servant," and "Ain't No Mo' Cane in Dis Brazis." As had become his custom, Wolff largely obscured the source tunes through esoteric methods of transformation.

Beyond that, he encrusted the results with quasi-severe techniques from the Middle Ages and the Renaissance: hocket, ornamented cantus firmus, and a general interweaving of lines, either stratified in some way (by character, normative rhythmic values, register) or equal voiced. Wolff further transforms his material by directing the players to interact in various ways beyond the mere note-to-note playing. Overall, the tones of the original tunes become seed crystals that Wolff grows (or allows to grow) in different directions from movement to movement—and, similarly, from piece to piece. The seeds have political associations via their titles, texts, and social contexts. But the crystalline growth Wolff generates hides those associations, leaving to titles and program notes their interpretation.

Wolff tended to specify dynamics less than other parameters. This came partly from his affinity with the Baroque, particularly his own keyboard playing of Bach and Frescobaldi. As in those cases, Wolff wanted his music not to have one fixed image that depended on a certain dynamic scheme. In other words, dynamics should be the last thing that shaped a composition. In early keyboard music, dynamics were simply determined by the instrument being used (e.g., harpsichord, organ). And in ensembles, historically, density determined dynamics. The number of players playing determined loudness or softness. But for Wolff, the larger the ensemble he chose, the less comfortable he felt leaving issues of *balance* to the players, especially given his constant mixing of vastly different types of instruments. One solution was to determine players' dynamics with respect to one another ("louder than the other players") or to the spectrum of possible dynamics ("as softly as possible"). Nevertheless, he tended to use flat dynamics only, leaving crescendo or diminuendo to the individual players' expressive sense.

But what to do with an orchestra?

Turning to the orchestra, of course, potentially meant Wolff would have to upend his earlier use of "orchestra" for any small ensemble and to return it to its traditional meaning, which implied instrumental families, homogeneous groups of timbres or conventional doublings and timbral blends. He also needed to lean away from the mutual cuing of his chamber groups toward something more decisive and autocratic, including the shaping of group dynamics through conventional symbols. One big question would be that of the *tutti*, that unique trait large ensembles possess to overwhelm the listener with the sheer mass of sound. That had been almost anathema to Wolff, who relied on spare, compact gestures juxtaposed, ones whose relative unassertiveness spurned stereotypical modernism.

Wolff had not studied orchestration and had no models of large-scale multitimbral craft that would guide a new orchestral composer. He rarely thought chordally or in long, developmental movements. Rather, he favored independent lines superimposed in miniatures. On the other hand, from his study with Cage, Wolff knew well Webern's op. 21 Symphony. It exemplified spare orchestral interweaving of lines as well as brevity, especially in the small variation segments of its second movement.

Wolff's earliest orchestral pieces took tentative steps into this new domain.[14] He wrote the first, *Exercise 23 (Bread and Roses)* (1983) for a competition. It didn't win and remains unpublished and unperformed. Its sequel, *Exercise 24*, returned to the same folk-song source via an orchestration of his four-hand piano piece, *Exercise 22 ("Bread and Roses for John")*. This work adapted the piano piece for a very small orchestra (single winds, with horns, trumpet, piano, and percussion), although the nature of the original almost defied any sense of melody or accompaniment. Instead, *Exercise 24* more or less "colorizes" *Exercise 22* by refraction, splitting lines and gestures into different (though usually blended) instrumental hybrids of color. Wolff also had another issue to contend with: the desynchronization of piano parts called for in the earlier work. He attempted a fairly literal translation of the effect by, at the proper times, having the players subdivide into two groups that would be conducted independently, though not straying too far apart in tempo.

In December 1986 Cage traveled to Japan for the premiere of his *Etcetera 2/4 Orchestras,* commissioned by the Suntory International Program for Music Composition. The Suntory beer company, which had given its name to a concert hall in Tokyo, had begun commissioning new orchestral pieces, each of which became the centerpiece for a program at the hall. That program would include the commissioned piece, the commissioned composer's choice of "older" classical orchestral pieces, and orchestral music by another living composer whom the commissioned composer regarded as congenial to his work. When commissioned, Cage chose Wolff to fulfill that latter role. At the time Wolff only had the one short orchestra piece to offer, *Exercise 24.* So he made a second one to go with it, titled with the African word *Liyashiswa.* This brief work for medium-sized orchestra (woodwinds in pairs, but including harp and two percussionists) alternated sections of material similar to his Peace Marches with melodic lines hocketed and cued from one instrument to the next via coordination neumes.

By the mid-1980s the New York School had begun to move from the fringes of modernism into the Western historical canon. From Wolff's fiftieth birthday (1984) onward, retrospective concerts and premieres of his new works sharply increased, most prominently in New York, London, Germany, and Japan (although ad hoc performances of his most indeterminate works, particularly *Edges,* the *Prose Collection* and the *Exercises* were harder to track). In 1988–89, Wolff received four paid commissions—the most he had received in that span of time so far. He also began to receive frequent grants from the Meet the Composer organization. In 1990 a section of *Burdocks* appeared in anthology intended for university music classes.[15] In 1993 and 1995, interviews with Wolff appeared in two books of conversations with important living composers.[16]

But the New York School had also begun to erode after the unexpected death of Morton Feldman at the age of sixty-four in 1987 and the death five years later of John Cage (weeks shy of his eightieth birthday).

Wolff's ideas had affected Cage's, as we have seen. But Wolff's earliest *music* had decisively influenced Feldman's late music. Though Wolff had long since abandoned his earliest pitch-restricted techniques in small pieces, Feldman had resurrected them. Both Bunita Marcus and Orlando Jacinto Garcia recall Feldman in his last years speaking admiringly of Wolff's Duo for Violins.[17] The evidence of its influence on Feldman is persuasive: time and again, Feldman begins a work with more than two minutes of a three- or four-pitch set, progressively varying its rhythms and timbres.[18]

In his last year, Feldman wrote a four-hour duo titled *For Christian Wolff* (1986), which he begins with a set of four half-step related pitches deployed among octaves and played in short polyrhythmic gestures for the work's first two pages—nearly five minutes of music. Although he did not learn of the piece until after Feldman died, Wolff himself could not miss the point of *For Christian Wolff*: "the connection with me was that [it] referred back to some of my earliest pieces, which were characterized by having a very small number of pitches. . . . For a long time, that's all you get is these pitches shifting back and forth. It's a gesture or recollection of the kind of music that I did early on."[19]

Wolff, in turn, wrote a piece for Feldman's death, *For Morty*, part of a growing list of pieces named for one or another friend, mentor, or hero, who was often connected with politics or political music.[20] By the mid-1990s these included *For Cornelius* [Cardew] (quartet, 1983), *Rosas* [Luxemburg and Parks] (duo, 1989–90), *Emma* [Goldman] (trio, 1989), *Ruth* [Crawford Seeger] (duo, 1991), *Malvina* [Reynolds] (solo, 1989; then duo, 1992), *For Si* [Kahn] (quintet, 1992), *Peggy* [Seeger] (solo or duo, 1993), and *Merce* [Cunningham] (1–9 players, 1993). *For Morty* used three instruments that evoked Feldman's often delicate ringing chords: vibraphone, glockenspiel, and piano. Through much of the piece, the resonant multiovertoned timbres combined with mechanistic rhythms to create a music box texture, though often a music box as if designed by Webern. The piece opens with uncharacteristically pandiatonic (i.e., "white-key") counterpoint, almost neo-Renaissance in its simplicity. Accidentals gradually increase, unleashing the texture from modality. The music thins and fades, succeeded by a section consisting of strongly asserted simultaneities (mostly trichords and tetrachords), the multicolored but simple-rhythmed kind that abounded in Webern's music. A brief, almost indifferent, solo line emerges, and then the piece more or less reprises the earlier material. The piece ends with a run of sixteenth notes over a chord of silently depressed piano keys spelling the musical letters in *Feldman* (F, E, D, A).

Wolff had wanted to make a piece for Cage's eightieth birthday in 1992. He had completed only about half of it when Cage died. Then, in 1996, an orchestral commission from the Donaueschingen Festival revived the piece in Wolff's mind. But on 13 August 1996, four years and one day after Cage, David Tudor died. In completing the work during the next two years, Wolff made it into a combined memorial titled *John, David.*

It had been preceded a year earlier by a kind of orchestral stepping-stone, *Spring*. In February 1995 the New Hampshire Symphony Orchestra (a young rival to the old New Hampshire Philharmonic) had offered Wolff two hundred dollars to write them a new work. Paid commissions still being a luxury, Wolff complied with *Spring*, an eighteen-minute, three-movement piece for Beethovenian orchestra (woodwinds in pairs, small string sections) but with three percussionists. It exemplified Wolff's reuse of materials, not just in its derivation of gestures from old melodies, but in its wholesale contrafacture (as in the Baroque): the first movement essentially orchestrates the third of Wolff's *Black Song Organ Preludes* of nine years earlier. The second movement is a collage of fragments, some intact, others revamped via well-established late-period techniques. As usual, the brevity of gestures bespeaks not so much pointillism as ellipticality, as though continuities, extensions of ideas, and transitions between them had been omitted, bypassed, or excised. It seemed at times almost a kind of sloganeering—or picket-signage—turned into music. Only the third movement delves into the contingent performance practice of the 1970s, with multiple chamber groups superimposed, players playing independently or interdependently. The autocracy of the conductor-tutti surrenders to the more progressive (and now common) Wolffian model: deployment of "chamber musics coexisting."[21]

The two parts of the weightier *John, David* each refer to its respective dedicatee and each use different methods. The "John" part originally was to have eighty "songs" in it, each containing from one to eighty notes, respectively. Their order, procedure (monophonic, heterophonic, or hocketed), and even superposition would then be determined by chance—one of the few times in his later work that Wolff used chance procedures, an overt homage to Cage on his birthday. Every set of ten songs would also have its own particular traits (1–9 = loud; 10–19 = short durations; and so forth). Before Cage's death Wolff had completed only thirty of these songs, of which sixteen were superimposed on other songs.

Meanwhile, the "David" part connected to Tudor more obliquely. When Wolff had told his percussionist friend Robyn Schulkowsky about this commission, she urged him to be careful of the orchestra, questioning their ability to handle his kind of scoring. "Probably your safest bet," Wolff recalls her saying, "is to write a concerto, because then you will be assured that at least the soloist has prepared their material beforehand."[22] So he devised an elaborate solo part for percussion for her. He conceived of it with the virtuosity of David Tudor in mind. The "David" of *John, David* has four distinct sections, the first three of which consist of short, scherzolike episodes. The first derives from the medieval English song "Westryn Wind"; the second uses (in the chordal passages of winds and brass) several shape-note hymns; the third spins its lines from the Depression-era song "Hallelujah, I'm a Bum." Throughout these sections, as is typical of Wolff's orchestral music, the orchestra is treated in a piecemeal way. But in the fourth section, everybody takes up an uncharacteristic (for Wolff) tutti of sustained sounds, producing a kind of wailing that one may hear as the formal lament of this memorial piece.

This last section uses a uniquely Wolffian version of recapitulation: he returns to a certain point in the piece, then collects pitches (not pitch classes, but pitches in their specific register), and begins playing them all again simultaneously: all E flats, for example, in their original durations, all Ds in their original durations, C sharps, Cs, and so on. Such a recapitulation begins extremely thickly, of course, but gradually thins as the different quantities and durations of pitches are used up. In this case, the end comes when only three pitches remain. From so rigorous an additive procedure these long-held notes in all registers come across as a massive, but plaintive, wail of grief. Moments such as this—however Apollonian the systematic means that generated them—differ so much from what surrounds them that there seems to be, for the first time in Wolff's music, a romantic sensibility.

But as dramatic as the effect might be, Wolff insists that his original intent was more surprise than drama. He surrenders the piece, in a way, to a mechanical procedure as part of his personal resistance to anything that seems like willful rhetoric, a convention that bothers him in most music since Beethoven: "It strikes me as rather overblown or pompous. It has a certain kind of hollowness to it. If it's really well done it can be very powerful and moving, but it needs to have some kind of mystery about it—where it's coming from and how it's acting. And that's what I try to do."[23]

As for the performance of *John, David* at Donaueschingen, Wolff described it in terms one often hears among contemporary composers: the orchestra was underrehearsed, the players indifferent, and the rendition "passable, but not a very happy experience."[24]

The year 1996, Wolff's twenty-fifth at Dartmouth, began with a university symposium and music festival in his honor, titled "Christian Wolff: The Composer and the Classicist": concerts, lectures, panel discussions, and even a booklet with a new retrospective essay by Wolff ("Sketch of a Statement"), a list of works, a discography, and a brief collation of statements by and about the composer-classicist. The title of the event uncharacteristically treated both prongs of his career equally. One panel discussion featured his colleagues in classics speaking of his contributions as a teacher and Greek scholar, particularly of the plays of Euripides. Pressed to identify the link between his Greek scholarship and adventurous music, Wolff balked. They were utterly separate. But was there a connection with the politics that fueled his more recent music? One of his colleagues thought Wolff saw in Euripides a protofeminism that resonated with Wolff's own.[25] Wolff himself, of course, in his first year at Dartmouth, had used Plato to connect politics to new music. Only years later would he find a deeper connection: "Grappling with that past, those tragic texts and their possible theatrical realization, in their difference, recalcitrance, and opaqueness, makes for a sense of openness and possibility."[26] Even so, one could be forgiven for not recognizing the Cageian experimentalist in Wolff's 1996–97 faculty productivity report, in which his goals included "Ongoing research on the social, political and legal history of Athens in the latter part of the fifth century BCE with a view to a book length study which would contextualize as fully as possible the dramatic treatment of the myth of Orestes' and Electra's revenge (on their mother and her lover for their father's death) in Sophocles' *Electra*, with additional literary contextualization in the surviving body of Attic tragedy (notably Aeschylus' and Euripides' versions of this mythic material)."[27]

The year closed with the announcement that Wolff had won the third biennial $50,000 John Cage Award given by the Foundation for Contemporary Performance Arts. He followed in a line of recipients clearly tied to Cage: the first, Tudor, and the second, Takahisa Kosugi, who since 1977 had been a resident composer-performer with Cunningham's dance troupe (the next recipient after Wolff would be Earle Brown). Asked what he would do with this sudden windfall, Wolff remarked, "I've got two kids on the way to college. Need I say more?"[28]

In 1998, MusikTexte published the first collection of Wolff's writings, a hefty softbound bilingual book with German on the left and English on the right. Though Wolff deemed many contenders for inclusion "unimportant" and "not necessary" for such a book, the final collation, *Cues*, gathered together thirty-eight articles and interviews about his own and others' work (though only one essay from his work as classicist), fifty-six program notes, his verbal scores (mainly the entire *Prose Collection*), a preface by Rzewski, and a work list that ended with *Pulse*, the trumpet and piano duo that followed *John, David*.

Compositionally, Wolff seemed to reach a new level of consolidation and refinement in *Pebbles* (1999), a duo for violin and piano written almost forty years after Wolff's previous duo for those instruments. The title was an acknowledgment that this is another collection of miniatures—though this time in homage to frequent miniaturist György Kurtág, whom Wolff had come to know and admire in the 1990s, calling him "that most poetic of composers."[29] Wolff found the instrumentation infelicitous, though. As he was writing the piece, he wrote to Rzewski that he was "going crazy trying to write for piano and violin!" But five days after that complaint, it was finished, though "whether or not it'll work I've no idea."[30]

His strategy: an extreme paring down of materials. The piece presents an elaborate dialogue-narrative in which the listener proceeds through twenty-four tableaus, ranging roughly from fifteen seconds to four minutes in putative clock time. Throughout the piece, the two instruments, as if speakers in a long, deepening conversation, continually restructure their relationship. For example, the piece begins with a kind of introduction in which each instrument seems to stake out for itself a distinct manner: the piano a florid solo bass line, the violin a brief pizzicato declamation. They then play in tandem, the piano in running sixteenth notes, the violin against it in bowed dotted eighths. Soon, in the piano's only two-voice utterance, the keyboard assumes both roles, after which the violin plays a long disjunct rhapsodic line above burbling groups of bass-clef sixteenths in the piano. In the sections that follow, we find long responsorial passages with piano and violin closely imitating each other in narrow-ranged stuttering eighth notes (and later in the piece, sixteenth notes); both instruments playing terse figures in similar motion; long soliloquies by the violin (first a prosaic arco, then, just before the work's final section, a chattering page of pizzicato); occasional short monologues by the piano; and so forth. Given the almost skeletal leanness of the lines and interactions between them, after the first four sections of the piece each subsequent one seems a transformation of one (or more) that preceded it. The spacious constellationlike closing page seems, paradoxically, both a culmination and a coda: by resembling none of the previous sections in gesture or texture, it seems an arrival at a new plateau and, at the same time, a digressive afterthought.

By the time Wolff wrote *Pebbles*, his virtuoso music of the previous two decades had been performed throughout Europe, Asia, and North America. In the 1990s alone he had written thirty-seven new works, almost all of which Peters had quickly put into print.[31] Digital technology now allowed for inexpensive audio reproduction and, via compact discs, widespread diffusion of new music and near-global awareness of even the New York School's most adventurous music. Thus, in the 1990s, fourteen different labels issued Wolff recordings, including Wergo, Vox, EMI, and the new labels HatArt and Mode, both of which specialized in recordings of avant-garde and experimental works. But the surprising coda to all this activity came with Wolff's crossover into rock.

In 1999, the alternative rock band Sonic Youth recorded *Goodbye 20th Century*, an album of experimental "classical" pieces that was conceived and coproduced by new music percussion virtuoso William (Willie) Winant and included Wolff's *Edges* and a movement from *Burdocks*. Those open scores would allow the group (augmented by Winant, Takehisa Kosugi, Christian Marclay, and Wolff himself) to work the pieces up in the studio, as rock groups typically did with their own music. Recording, of course, had always transgressed the intended variability of indeterminate scores, fixing one version into an implicitly authentic rendition of an "open" work. At the same time, multiple takes and tape splicing had allowed players and even composers to construct an artificial, semi-idealized recorded performance from a variety of actual in-studio performances. While not accustomed to playing Wolff scores, Sonic Youth could provide some of the best miking, editing, and mastering Wolff had encountered.

Although the album was hardly a mass-market success, it became something of a cult favorite as Sonic Youth (and Winant) toured western Europe playing the strange repertoire of *Goodbye 20th Century.* This set a new standard for the adjective "alternative" in alternative rock. And suddenly Christian Wolff (as with Varèse when promoted by Frank Zappa in the 1960s) became a minor rock star, with fresh name recognition among the college crowd of his children's generation—while at the same time his own generation remained mostly indifferent to this music that Rzewski had aptly said revealed "life's unpredictability."

7 Among Friends, in a Private World

ON 2 JULY 2002, EARLE BROWN DIED. That event left Wolff in a new role: he was now the last surviving member of the so-called New York School of composers. For many that made him the last ambassador for a latter-day tradition that Cage had constructed and whose first generation was now about to conclude. Four decades earlier Wolff had foreshadowed the creative box in which he might now find himself: in his dissertation he explains that he would show "the various expressions of the notion of survival, its ramifications and conditions, in [Euripides'] later plays." "Private survival," he notes, "conflicts with efforts to save a community," that group that provides "a sense of order" to living. But amid this dialectic, Euripides suggests, life is still "a form of exile which is resolved only among friends, in a private world."[1]

For Wolff, surviving his New York School colleagues—or, more to the point, some of his closest friends—had its professional detriments. He might be pegged as a merely *recherché* artist, a relic of an outmoded era. Consider the underlying bias in reviews such as this from the *New York Times* in 2008: Wolff's *For 1, 2, or 3 People* was "a static hodgepodge of miscellaneous avant-gardisms [that] felt like listening to the party bore who entertains only himself."[2] The growing dismissal of experimental composers such as Wolff partly reflected the press's waning attention to "classical" music itself, as well as the gradual overwhelming of modernism by neoromanticism, postmodernism, and, generally, greater "listener friendliness" than, even in his more determinate and less overtly political music, Wolff could offer. At the same time, the bad press may have reflected the sometimes cavalier performances of Wolff's earlier music. He had said in 1993 that "I am not . . . unduly anxious about the specific identity of any given piece, though some element of recognition, especially if combined with elements of surprise, is usually a pleasure."[3] Since some of those works had now entered the new-music canon, more and more players whom Wolff didn't know played the pieces under circumstances he couldn't oversee (the case in the *For 1, 2, or 3 People* performance critiqued above), leading to interpretations far looser than the scores' instructions required. This problem had begun at least as early as 1974, with the Julius Eastman–led performance of *Burdocks* in Carnegie Hall, whose slapstick histrionics and sonic "twiddles and twaddles" provoked sustained chuckling from the audience for fifteen minutes.[4]

On the other hand, survival offered its laurels. In 2005 he was inducted into the American Academy of Arts and Sciences. New recordings kept appearing, one of which *Wire* magazine noted on its list of the fifty best albums of 2006.[5] Wolff's new almost patriarchal status got him more attention than when his New York School colleagues thrived and he still worked as a professor. His "last-surviving-member" status headlined his billing at various events, for which he received an increasing number of invitations. Interviews and retrospective articles proliferated as he became the archivist and even archaeologist of not only his own, personal, history but that of U.S. experimental music. Meanwhile, as a bona fide elder statesman of the avant garde, he could guest lecture from the most eclectic musical sources he wished. Consider his reading list for the Some Music Issues class during his 2006 visiting professorship at the California Institute of the Arts: four books by Arthur C. Danto, two books apiece by Theodor Adorno and Alain Badiou, one each by John Ashbery, T. J. Clark, Nicholas Cook, Carl Dahlhaus, John Dewey, George Leonard, Meyer Shapiro, "anything by John Cage," and a recent collection of essays on, yes, the New York School.[6]

He also received more requests and commissions for new works. The first decade of the twenty-first century turned out to be the most prolific of Wolff's career: from 2000 though 2010 he wrote almost sixty new works—nearly half the number he had written during the previous forty years. Finding more time to compose, he consistently worked on one piece while planning or mentally outlining two or three more. But though he was unquestionably an *American* experimentalist, Wolff had almost always found more receptive audiences abroad. He routinely traveled long distances to premieres, the large majority of them in Europe.

Wolff the world traveler seemed the complete alter ego of the Wolff of domestic private life. Each summer, one could find him helping bring in the hay and doing other chores on the Royalton farm (both of Holly's parents having passed away, she now managed the farm). An avid family man, he had always helped the children with homework (especially in foreign languages), even through their college years. Amid paying bills, gardening, and cooking, he had gone with Holly and their four children to countless theater, dance, and musical performances, including, to the kids' occasional chagrin, those sparsely attended, puzzling new music concerts with Christian's own music on the program. The children noted his broad curiosity about sound in everything from testing the tone quality of car parts to expounding on musical craft in show tunes by Richard Rodgers. He freely voiced to his children his views on current events but kept much of his polemicism to himself—though, according to daughter Tamsen, "bad political news is one of the few things that can make him visibly upset."[7] His fatherly influence on all four children was, by all accounts, kindly but deep. Tristram explains that he learned from both parents the value of "the good work, the good fight [and] being part of a tradition, or being a nexus of many traditions, whose common thread is change."[8]

The orchestral pieces Wolff wrote in the opening decade of the twenty-first century amply display the multiplicity and diversity, complication and juxtaposition of techniques and structures that were now second nature. The provocateur of these large-scale works was the Czech-born composer and conductor Petr Kotik, who had known and championed the music of New York School composers for decades. Although he had premiered Wolff's *Nine* in 1963 in Prague, he had a particular fondness for the "interactive" scores of Wolff ever since he himself had played at the Burdocks Festival in 1972. The director of the S.E.M. Ensemble in New York since 1970, he also began the Ostrava Days Festivals in the Czech Republic in 2001. Held in odd-numbered years, they have featured Wolff as guest composer and lecturer each time. As of this writing, Wolff has written four orchestral (or multiorchestral) pieces for Kotik.

For an event in 1999, Kotik had decided to program Stockhausen's *Gruppen* for three orchestras, augmented his regular Czech orchestra in order to perform it, and booked performances in Prague and Berlin. Since he had the setup for three orchestras—including three conductors and three stages—and *Gruppen* is only around twenty minutes long, he asked Wolff and Alvin Lucier to compose new three-orchestra pieces. Suddenly massive instrumental forces became available to Wolff. But, investing the time required for such a work, Wolff wanted to compose one that would have a life beyond its premiere. (He also wanted it not to resemble *John, David.*) Returning to the spirit of *Burdocks*, Wolff composed *Ordinary Matter*, a work whose title celebrated the small percentage of cosmic material perceptible via the human senses. This piece has, he said, "hardly any score at all."[9] Only one section was scored for all players, the other fourteen scored for subsets of the orchestra, or available to any players. Some sections he called parasitic, in that each requires another section to be played with it.

To enhance clarity, Wolff reduces the number of players from *Gruppen*'s 109 to 80, cutting the number of percussionists in half and omitting cellos altogether (based on a *St. Matthew Passion* performance without cellos he had recently heard). He then makes the orchestras a well of possible textures. The counterpoint results mainly from loose, indeterminate parts, yielding juxtapositions or superpositions of tangled sound masses. Yet even with its multiple ensembles, which would typically provoke extreme polyphony, *Ordinary Matter* contains many passages where the music finds rhythmic and textural niches in which to linger for longer stretches than in many of his other works.[10]

There are fifteen sections, which in some cases overlap and span a spectrum from all three orchestras playing simultaneously to a transparent duo for harps. On one hand, a selection of players (up to the whole orchestra) may make very long sustained quiet sounds. On the other hand, all three orchestras may have very exact rhythmic procedures to follow, but the pitches remain unspecified (other than by a line to show relative height). Players must observe only the melodic contour. One section has a short stretch of solo material for everybody in the orchestras: eighty lines of solo material with the instruction that each player must play his or her twenty- or twenty-five-second line anywhere within the allotted three minutes. Wolff expects each instrumentalist to execute that task with keen alertness to the whole: "If they have a little bit of a conscience they will try not to destroy something that's going on quietly, or try to play quietly with it . . . the way you would in improvisation."[11]

Various types of controls demarcate the sections. The first section, extrapolated from a solo-line piece he had written for Alvin Lucier's seventieth birthday, has melodic material adding up to seventy notes. The whole orchestra reads the material in the instruments' own clefs and transpositions. This yields a variety of canonic transpositions and thus harmonic density, richly deployed over the span of three orchestras on the stage—with trumpet 1, for example, being dozens of yards away from trumpet 3. Rhythms tend to be free, with some note values prescribed, but relative tempi left open; durations of breaths sometimes constrain the length of phrases; the techniques of composing these lines derive from common Wolffian schemes (especially the loops-on-a-grid concept). The second section presents a variation on the first (again with seventy notes); a later section, which opens with the melody of a Shaker hymn, is scored for violins alone; two sections consist of prose instructions only; another section consists of four chords, each with fifteen notes, played by thirteen instruments (strings play double stops); and so forth. The whole piece, however, is modular: the conductor may use as much or as little of the collection as he or she wants. With the unlikelihood of marshaling three orchestras for more than this one occasion, Wolff wanted to ensure that some portions of the work could survive beyond it. Thus, a *minimum* performance could, in fact, be just the harp duet. Each of the sections remains relatively consistent, yielding a more or less self-contained piece.

The following year Kotik invited Wolff to write a smaller work for his S.E.M. chamber orchestra in New York. For this, Wolff returned to his peace march genre, which was now an almost reflexive act of his musical personality—especially with the backdrop of the second American war in Iraq. The title *Peace March 8*, said Wolff, refers to "the better choice, which must be declared ('March'). And especially when the other choice is about acquiring (yet more) power, because of, say, oil, which is despicable, at massive cost, not least of human life, not to mention humanity."[12] The work unfolds as a kind of concerto grosso, a gallery of quasi-bravado moments replete with assertive repeated-note fragments, some drawn from peace songs. Within an eclectic pitch vocabulary, it echoes vernacular bands (even fife and drum corps), anthems, and chorales via small ensembles, duos, even solo passages. The last section presents a variation on Hanns Eisler's four-part round, "Song for Peace," ending with a long oboe duo—this occurred to Wolff at the last minute, he said. Somehow, the piece needed a severe stripping down after twenty minutes of so much activity—especially the dense Eislerian round and the florid solo sections, said Wolff, which made the final duo "a nice, contrasting (simplifying, clarifying) conclusion." It was "a bit like a final chorale."[13]

The composer and the conductor sparred, though, on matters of notational determinacy. Wolff wanted the open procedures left more spontaneous; Kotik, as conductor, wanted more planning and up-front decisions. "The 'culture' of a standard orchestra doesn't sit well with contingency," Wolff wrote. "It's all about hierarchical control."[14] That tension lingered into 2005, when Wolff produced his most imposing one-orchestra work yet with the hypergeneric title *Orchestra: Pieces*. It is another suite of small movements (five), each characterized by its own texture (or textures): the first opening with free-floating winds and strings (fermatas over every note); the second with fast, loud, terse fanfaring followed by large juxtaposed blocks of sonority; the third, a violin solo with sparse chamber accompaniment; the fourth, mostly aphoristic calls and responses, including some of his densest multioctave doubling yet; and the fifth slowly evolving into another Tallis-influenced sound mass.

In 2009's *Rhapsody* for three chamber orchestras, the title manifests itself in the mood swings of its bold juxtapositions rather than in the sustained lyricism the title might imply. What most stands out in the work, though, is Wolff's ultimate tutti: more than thirty measures (189–221) in which all three orchestras play a single, mostly conjunct, treble line in unison. This passage—one of many where multiple doublings thicken an ambling line via romantic-style blended timbres—appears quite suddenly in the midst of his typical patchwork quilt of textures and moods. And for the first time in his work, a long solo line arguably becomes the dramatic center of the piece.

What is least accessible about these four orchestral works is their angularity of line and elliptical phrasing. What is most accessible is their miniaturist sectionalism, reminiscent of, say, the second movement of Webern's op. 21. In any case, they have made more inroads into orchestral programming in Europe than in the United States, constrained as the latter is by conservatism and a preference for flashy, coloristic textures or overtly neoromantic themes. Wolff's relative austerity in these works refutes the current trends in his own (adopted) homeland.

Music historians often gravitate toward large-ensemble pieces, as if size of forces constituted musical weight. But one cannot overlook Wolff's twenty-first-century works for smaller groups, even solos. He frequently returns, for example, to the piano. After a number of shorter pieces or collections of miniatures in the early 2000s, Wolff received in 2004 a commission to write a piece of approximately an hour in duration, but not using multiple movements. Wolff, however, did not want to craft a set of variations, even one as eclectic as Rzewski's *The People United.* So in *Long Piano*, Wolff constructed what will probably be his largest solo piano piece, a virtuoso anthology of ninety-five fragmentary sections, most of which seem to echo (or even quote) a portion of some earlier piano piece of his. More a compendium than a quilt, this work is perhaps the closest thing we have to an encyclopedia of late-Wolff habits and predilections:

long, widely spaced compound solo lines
two-voice counterpoint in synchronized equal note values (usually eighth notes)
stuttering repeated-note lines
hocketed lines spread across registers
rhythmically stratified two-voice counterpoint (i.e., longer notes against shorter notes)
block chords in syncopated quasi-chorales
restricted-pitch segments (e.g., no. 27) that closely resemble his earliest works

Such textures and arrays unfold mostly in *conventional* notation (though often with wedges for indeterminate rests, as had become Wolff's custom). The main breach with conventional notation is the work's opening, which begins with a set of neumes for fingers, not keys. (This was tagged on as a kind of prelude after he had written the rest and found that the piece was still too short in clock time.) The sections favor hyperchromatic pitch vocabulary, though interspersed with alternative pitch collections—even diatonic ones (e.g., the white-key section, no. 31). While the composition and ordering of the segments was mainly intuitive, in at least one area of the piece he used an 11×11 magic square to set up the proportions and durations of eleven sections of the piece.[15] Whatever the methods, the effect is grandly prismatic: one detects faint echoes of Rzewski's textural and idiomatic encyclopedism in *The People United*, the "all-over" jaggedness of Stockhausen's *Klavierstücke*, the broad canvases of late Feldman, and fleeting allusions to Schoenberg, Ives, Glass, and, of course, Wolff's own teenage music. Rzewski's response to the piece was simple: "right up my alley."[16]

If his orchestra works aspire to the tutti and piano works to the solo virtuosic, Wolff's chamber works—of which dozens more appeared in this decade, some again for open instrumentation—usually return to what listeners and players know best about his work: a hyperconscious reactivity among performers prompted by his notations and instructions. The original set of fourteen exercises (1974) had initiated a new strategy of chamber music upon which subsequent exercises expanded. The set of twenty-two *Microexercises* (2006) distills Wolff's methods of coaxing music from avid performers.

Generally, no more than one hundred sounds were to be made within each microexercise. The most common notational layouts are monophonic (solo) lines or two-voice counterpoint. The most common variables are tempo, dynamics, order of events, and number of players, with open clefs and octave doublings or transpositions left to the players. A few microexercises, though, stand out: one a slow melody with percussion accompaniment; a four-part round; a two-voice hocket; and four that uses the time notations he had not used for more than forty years. The compositional methods he used for these distilled pieces include methodical transposition of pitches in folk melodies, partial rhythmic imitation, recycling and permutation of notes in previous pieces in the set, general reworking of previous pieces in the set, and systematic gestural reordering: that is, taking a series of terse gestures, numbering them (e.g., 1, 2, 3, 4, 5, 6, 7, 8, 9) and then recasting them both ends against the middle (1, 9, 2, 8, 3, 7, 4, 6, 5), possibly with some free reordering (he calls these pattern breaks) along the way (e.g., 1, 9, 2,

8, 3, 7, 5, 4, 6). Except for some genuinely free intuitive counterpoint here and there, Wolff usually uses some sort of calculative process to arrive at his choices or constraints, even if he later forgets what they were. That allowance of forgetting, indeed, he values as a way of not feeling bound by attempts to avoid self-repetition: not knowing if you've already used a method allows it to seem fresh in your mind each time.

After all these years, has a distinctive Christian Wolff "voice" emerged? English critics sometimes speak of "thumbprints," as in, "so and so's thumbprint is evident in this or that work." A thumbprint is the kind of expressive presence that immediately identifies say, Shostakovich, or Stravinsky, or Ives, or others. Wolff happily recalls that David Behrman said two things about Wolff's music: it was *honest* and it was *funny*. What accounts for the "honesty," Wolff believes, is a lack of pretense. The music is unassuming, even unimpressive. It contains little obvious rhetoric, lacks the "in-your-face" assertiveness that characterizes modernism. Wolff puts it bluntly: "I notice that when I go to a concert and my music is there with somebody else's, I think, 'Boy, look at that piece. It makes my music look as if I don't know what I'm doing, or that I could use some composition lessons or something.' I don't mind that at all, but it is quite striking, in some cases the contrast between very elegantly constructed pieces full of flash and color [while] mine seems very drab." As for the "funny" aspect: "I won't set out to be funny, but if something comes out humorous I'm quite pleased with that; I'll let that be. And in some ways it's a fine line. It's peculiar—or *quirky*, I guess, is a good word for it."[17]

Certainly Wolff's works make one-way trips. He avoids projecting reminiscences or recurrences for their own sake. For Wolff, progressive music needs to reject recapitulation and, indeed, any sense of "arch" in the trajectory of the form. (Bartók's arch forms, he remarked, seemed to "run against the grain of music which moves through time.")[18] Although Wolff's classic (i.e., best-known) work relies on concept, performance practice, or political messaging, the large-scale late works depend more and more on *montage*, the aesthetic friction of juxtaposing small contrasting movements. By the twenty-first century it became clear that Wolff's long pieces would be mosaics, profuse suites of shorter movements, often miniatures, played without interruption.

Still, in the latest works, Wolff seems to work intuitively toward and achieve some sort of organicism, however tenuous. It is true that, in some ways, organic consistency permeated even the earliest works. In those works, by severely limiting pitch, no matter what presumed discontinuity he injected into the ordering of sections, the result seemed highly coherent. By paring down his materials he could stay confident that sense would emerge. "I approach piecemeal material with the greatest attention, figuring that, if it's as well made as I can make it, each bit for itself (and using usually individual systemic procedures), the stitching together of these bits will somehow add up."[19]

Despite his habitual compositional routines and their prolific results since 2000, Wolff says he has yet to find his "groove": "I admired the late Feldman and Cage because it looked, from the outside, like they got into these grooves where they just turned out masses of music. I haven't been able to do that yet, so every piece is a struggle. The pieces do seem to keep coming, you know, three, four, or five a year. But it's still hard work." The restlessness inside some of his pieces is mirrored in the restlessness between pieces. "It's this hope that I will think of something new to do. . . . I usually don't, but just having that as a possibility" propels him forward.[20] The evolution of Wolff's style has mirrored that of style periods, generally: to paraphrase Dahlhaus's formulation, one finds more extreme stylization at the front end, more eclecticism at the back end.[21]

Perhaps unsurprisingly, in his later years Wolff has taken more and more interest in *endings*. While sections of a work often end unresolved, the whole work must have in Wolff's view a decisive ending beyond the mere cessation of sound. "What comes out (what turns out to be) the end of a piece gets (from the listener, as well as composer and performers) a particular kind of attention, simply by virtue of being at the end, the last thing you hear/do at that point."[22] One sees that impulse in the striking endings of most of the orchestral pieces or of *Long Piano*, with its brief final quotation of a traditional round ("Dona Nobis Pacem"). Nevertheless, to end a piece is not to deem it finished. Wolff often recalls Cage's teaching him that no piece is complete until it has been performed. In making new musical objects, one may accumulate piles of sketchbooks and scores. But they still require playing to "exist" fully as *pieces of music*.

Wolff may be the exemplary *homo ludens*, "Man the player," as Johan Huizinga labels our species, play being its object and design. As a young man, Wolff recalls, "I wasn't really into books. I was a jock."[23] As a doctoral student he chose to study the plays of Euripides. As a composer he created almost theaterlike games, interplays of performers' roles and behaviors. The idea of "playing" answered two of Wolff's deepest concerns: freedom and learning. Even when guided by rules, playing is freedom. The term *experiment* seems to connote something more rigorous and goal driven. But as Huizinga famously wrote, "Let my playing be my learning, and my learning be my playing."[24] That playing-as-learning defined one fundamental of what had come to be known as experimental music. Just so, Wolff's most potent gift to the world of composition comes in those scores in which he insists that players *play*, with all the word's hints of gamesmanship, strategy, deftness, and attention.

Figure 10. Christian Wolff at the University of Northern Colorado, March 2010. Photo by Joseph F. Haefeli. Used by permission.

So to end this survey of Wolff's life and work we give a final nod to Wolff the player—with apologies for the verbal redundancy to make a point: one thinks back to his time at Friends Seminary, playing duos with David Lewin, then to his continual playing in his own and others' works through the years, his ad hoc playing during his experimental music courses and, in turn, in guest residencies at other schools, playing with Cardew and the AMM in the late 1960s, ongoing playing (and recording) with British friends such as Eddie Prevost and John Tilbury, and his private (and occasionally public) playing with Dartmouth colleagues Larry Polansky and Kui Dong. Most of this playing has been, in some way or another, improvisational.

Improvising has invigorated the composer as he approaches his eightieth year. He improvises regularly on piano and melodica, vocalizes in various ways, makes delicate noises on available surfaces, always drawing from his private lexicon of ideas. If one can listen profusely, Wolff seems to do so just that, inserting mostly tentative, fragmentary, monophonic gestures into the texture. Or consider this strategy: if "it's gotten very loud and my feeling is that it's too loud, it's too much. . . . I'm allowed to stop playing entirely, or play very, very quietly, nearly inaudibly, until someone can hear what I'm doing."[25] He approaches the task of improvisation with an enormous store of developmental strategies and previously written fragments in his mind and hands. "When he improvises," says Willie Winant, "it's like he's playing his own music."[26] Even so, much of his improvisation, particularly with Polansky and Kui Dong, attempts a blank slate: "It's better not to know [what you're going to do]. And it's impossible to rehearse. In some way that's an attraction. You just have to sort of jump in and see what happens."[27]

Improvisation keeps music in what may be its most fragile, even vulnerable mode. "The glory of it and the disaster of it," he says, "is that you do it and it's gone."[28] That speaks to our times, Wolff believes: "The state of the world is alarmingly tentative, seems more than ever on the brink. Can music be anything else?"[29]

Reflecting on Wolff, Polansky said that "because of Christian's humility, he may get the short end of the stick, more so than someone who's put on a lot more airs. But he's just one of the band, really, and that's all he really wants to be: just a musician playing music. He doesn't pretend to be anything other than that."[30] In the end, that may be the mystery behind Wolff's achievements as a scholar and composer: it is all a kind of profound playing in both the primal and advanced senses that Huizinga articulated. And for the "last surviving member" of the New York School, the ability to keep playing may be the greatest blessing. Life, as Wolff detected in Euripides, remains "a form of exile which is resolved only among friends, in a private world." But within that private world of friends, Wolff concluded, "survival is for happiness and pleasure."[31]

NOTES

Introduction

1. Since writing this, we gratefully witnessed the appearance of the first scholarly book on Wolff's music, a handsome collection of essays (to which one of the present authors contributed): Stephen Chase and Philip Thomas, eds., *Changing the System: The Music of Christian Wolff* (Surrey, U.K.: Ashgate, 2010).

2. Christian Wolff, *Cues: Writings and Conversations* (Köln, Germany: MusikTexte, 1998), 104.

3. Cole Gagne, *Soundpieces 2: Interviews with American Composers* (Metuchen, N.J.: Scarecrow Press, 1993), 447.

4. Wolff, *Cues*, 154. See also the discussion in Mark D. Nelson, "Social Dynamics at the Heart of Composition: Implications of Christian Wolff's Indeterminate Music," *Contemporary Music Forum* 1 (1989): 3–14.

5. Frederic Rzewski to Wolff, 10 October 1985, in Wolff's personal archive, which he kindly shared with the authors. Hereafter cited as Wolff Papers.

Chapter 1. Orpheus in Tennis Sneakers

1. Kurt Wolff quoted by Helen Wolff (at min. 6:32) in the Richard Kaplan documentary film *The Exiles* (Connoisseur Home Video, 1989).

2. Kurt Wolff quoted in Michael Ermarth, ed., *Kurt Wolff: A Portrait in Essays and Letters*, trans. Deborah Lucas Schneider (Chicago: University of Chicago Press, 1991), 19.

3. Kurt Wolff quoted by Helen Wolff (at min. 1:49:16) in *The Exiles*.

4. For the Wolff family chronology, see Günter Grass and Helen Wolff, *Briefe 1959–1994*, ed. Daniela Hermes (Göttingen, Germany: Steidl, 2003), 555–61.

5. On the history of Pantheon, see Steven John Schuyler, "Kurt Wolff and Hermann Broch: Publisher and Author in Exile" (PhD dissertation, Harvard University, 1984).

6. Helen Wolff (at min. 1:00:36) in *The Exiles*.

7. Barbara Weidle, "Hard Work—Determination," (interview in German with Christian Wolff), in Barbara Weidle, ed., *Kurt Wolff: Ein Literat und Gentleman* (Bonn, Germany: Weidle Verlag, 2007), 169–79 (Hicks's translation). Other information here is also from Weidle.

8. Wolff to Michael Hicks, email 29 April 2008.

9. Ibid.; Calvert Watkins, interview by Michael Hicks, 3 June 2008.

10. Christian Wolff, "Music—Experiment—Education," *Sonus* 26, no. 1 (Fall 2005): 20. Wolff's visits to jazz clubs are detailed in Watkins, interview by Hicks.

11. Wolff, interview by Hicks, 27 March 2010.

12. Watkins, interview by Hicks.

13. "Morton Feldman Slee Lecture, April 15, 1973," ublib.buffalo.edu/libraries/units/music/spcoll/feldman/mfslee326.html (accessed 21 February 2006).

14. Jean-Jacques Nattiez, ed., *The Boulez-Cage Correspondence*, trans. and ed. Robert Samuels (Cambridge and New York: Cambridge University Press, 1993), 56–57.

15. Ibid., 55.

16. Wolff has talked often about the assignments Cage gave him. See, for example, Cole Gagne, *Soundpieces 2: Interviews with American Composers* (Metuchen, N.J.: Scarecrow Press, 1993), 444–45; William Duckworth, *Talking Music: Conversations with John Cage, Philip Glass, Laurie Anderson, and Five Generations of American Experimental Composers* (New York: Schirmer Books, 1995), 185–86.

17. Christian Wolff, "Experimental Music around 1950 and Some Consequences and Causes (Social-Political and Musical)," *American Music* 27 (Winter 2009): 426.

18. David Patterson, "Cage and Beyond: An Annotated Interview with Christian Wolff," *Perspectives of New Music* 32 (1994): 61.

19. Kyle Gann explains nicely the appeal of gamuts: "Limitation of sonorities aids in creating the identity of a piece, and allows the composer to create meaning without relying on syntax analogous to the tonal system. It can also be a kind of second-order composing, working with more evolved sonorities instead of individual notes, which can get kind of tiring." Reply to "ALS," 14 July 2008, in comment thread for Gann's "Wheels Turning," www.artsjournal.com/postclassic/2008/07/wheels_turning.html (accessed 5 October 2008).

20. Five works written in the twelve months after the Duo for Violins have been withdrawn or lost by Wolff: Song (for voice, trumpet and trombone), Suite in Four Parts (for flute and violin), an untitled work for flute, clarinet, and violin (not to be confused with the Serenade from this period), *In the Beginning* (for two percussionists), and *It Being Christmas* (for percussion). One of note from this period, recently published but seemingly unrelated to any of these other works in its technique is the *Madrigals* for three voices, which abandoned specified pitch altogether: Wolff specified the rhythms and phonemes, but represented pitch only by distance above or below a center line representing a comfortable midrange for each respective singer.

21. The composition of that trio is discussed in David Nicholls, "Getting Rid of the Glue: The Music of the New York School," in Steven Johnson, ed., *The New York Schools of Music and the Visual Arts* (New York: Routledge, 2001), 39–41.

22. Nattiez, *Boulez-Cage Correspondence*, 108.

23. This and the following quotes in this paragraph are from Cage, *Silence*, 71–72.

24. Wolff to Michael Hicks, email 25 September 2008.

25. John Cage to David Tudor, undated letter (ca. October 1951), David Tudor Papers, Getty Research Institute, Special Collections.

26. Wolff, interview by Michael Hicks, 9 March 2006.

27. Pierre Boulez to John Cage (with handwritten note by Christian Wolff), summer 1951, in Nattiez, *Boulez-Cage Correspondence*, 97.

28. Wolff also refers to nine dynamics and nine "rhythmic configurations," though these seem less apparent.

29. Morton Feldman, *Give My Regards to Eighth Street: Collected Writings of Morton Feldman*, ed. B. H. Friedman (Cambridge, Mass.: Exact Change, 2000), 119.

30. *For the Birds: John Cage in Conversation with Daniel Charles* (Boston: Marion Boyars, 1981; originally published in French, 1976),

31. Austin Clarkson traces the English publication history of the *I Ching* in David Bernstein and Christopher Hatch, eds., *Writings through John Cage's Music, Poetry and Art* (Chicago: University of Chicago Press, 2001), 84–86.

32. Duckworth, *Talking Music*, 188.

33. Richard Kostelanetz, comp. and ed., *John Cage, Writer: Previously Uncollected Pieces* (New York: Limelight, 1993), 72.

34. John Cage to Helen Wolff, "12.E.17" [1954], reprinted in *Musik Texte* 106 (August 2005): 48–49.

35. "A Chance Encounter with Christian Wolff" (Interview with Frank J. Oteri, 11 January 2002), www.newmusicbox.org/35/interview_wolff.pdf (accessed 21 February 2006), sec. 3 ("Interpreting Indeterminate Music"). In the same source: "I still had those paramenters, and I still had to go to school during the day and stuff like that! So to that extent, clearly we were in a slightly different world."

36. Feldman, *Give My Regards to Eighth Street*, 16.

Chapter 2. Situations of Too Extreme Difficulty: 1951–1959

1. See "Two Composers on American Music at Mid-Century: Walter Piston in Conversation with Wilfrid Mellers, 1962," *American Music* 28 (Spring 2010): 123–24.

2. For an overview of Wolff's piano writing, see Philip Thomas, "For Pianist: The Solo Piano Music," in Stephen Chase and Philip Thomas, eds., *Changing the System: The Music of Christian Wolff* (Surrey, U.K.: Ashgate, 2010), 51–91.

3. Those brief essays appeared in the short-lived New York journal *Trans/formation* (1952). Wolff's contribution is reprinted in Christian Wolff, *Cues: Writings and Conversations* (Köln, Germany: MusikTexte, 1998), 20–22.

4. "Tudor Tries Hand at Experimenting," *New York Times*, 2 January 1952, 20.

5. "J. B.," "Look, No Hands! And It's 'Music,'" *New York Times*, 15 April 1954.

6. Steven John Schuyler, "Kurt Wolff and Hermann Broch: Publisher and Author in Exile" (PhD dissertation, Harvard University, 1984), 79.

7. David Tudor to Karlheinz Stockhausen, 4 November 1955, in Imke Misch and Markus Bandur, *Karlheinz Stockhausen bei den Internationalen Ferienkursen für Neue Musik in Darmstadt 1951–1996: Dokumente und Briefe* (Kürten, Germany: Stockhausen-Stiftung für Musik, 2001), 115. Hereafter cited as Misch and Bandur, *Dokumente und Briefe*.

8. Wolff to John Cage, 5 February [1956], John Cage Collection, Northwestern University Library. Hereafter cited as Cage Collection.

9. John Cage to Wolff, 28 March 1956, Wolff Papers; Wolff to Cage, 8 April 1956, Cage Collection.

10. "Frederic Rzewski Visits America: A Conversation with Frank J. Oteri @ Nonesuch Records, NYC on John Cage's Birthday (September 5, 2002)," 2, at http://newmusicbox.org/43/rzewski_interview.pdf (accessed 11 February 2011).

11. See his comments in "On December 1952," *American Music* 26 (Spring 2008): 1–12.

12. "Christian Wolff Seminar (an excerpt)." From *Ostrava Days 2003 Report* at www.ocnmh.cz/days2003_lectures_wolff.htm (accessed 11 February 2011).

13. Ibid.

14. There is some uncertainty on Wolff's part as to the chronology here, i.e., to what extent the "prototype" piece he prepared with Rzewski for performance in spring 1957 actually was or became the Duo 1 score whose fair copy is dated (and was premiered) in December 1957.

15. John Holzaepfel, "Reminiscences of a Twentieth-Century Pianist: An Interview with David Tudor," *Musical Quarterly* 78 (1994): 636.

16. Tudor writes about an "incident" between Cage and Boulez on this issue—an episode of the growing breach between the two composers—in a letter to Stockhausen, 12 March 1957, in Misch and Bandur, *Dokumente und Briefe*, 162.

17. John Cage to Wolff, 18 April 1960, Wolff Papers.

18. "Interview with Roger Reynolds, 1962," in Elliott Schwartz and Barney Childs, eds., *Contemporary Composers on Contemporary Music* (New York: Holt, Rinehart and Winston, 1967), 340.

19. John Cage, *A Year from Monday* (Middletown, Conn.: Wesleyan University Press, 1969), 136.

20. John Cage, *Silence* (Middletown, Conn.: Wesleyan University Press, 1961), 38.

21. "Interview with Roger Reynolds, 1962," 340.

22. "John Cage and Roger Reynolds: A Conversation," *Musical Quarterly* 65 (October 1979): 582–83.

23. For a discussion of Tudor's score preparation, see John Holzaepfel, "David Tudor and the Performance of American Experimental Music 1950–1959" (PhD dissertation, City University of New York, 1994).

24. Holzaepfel, "Reminiscences of a Twentieth-Century Pianist," 636.

25. Carolyn Brown, *Chance and Circumstance: Twenty Years with Cage and Cunningham* (New York: Knopf, 2007), 39.

26. Frederic Rzewski to Wolff, letter 9 August 1959, Wolff Papers, original emphasis.

27. Frederic Rzewski to Wolff, letter 21 August 1959, Wolff Papers.

28. Doris Hering, quoted in Brown, *Chance and Circumstance*, 253, emphasis on the word *sparsely* added.

29. Cornelius Cardew, "Notation: Interpretation, Etc.," *Tempo* 58 (Summer 1961): 21–23.

30. Cornelius Cardew quoted in John Tilbury, *Cornelius Cardew (1936–1981): A Life Unfinished* (Essex, U.K.: Copula, 2008), 89.

31. Wolff to John Cage and Merce Cunningham, July [date water damaged, but 1959], Cage Collection.

Chapter 3. Vast, Sparse Areas of Possibility: 1960–1969

1. Burdette C. Stampley, "To Whom It May Concern," letter 20 April 1961, Wolff Papers.

2. Originally published in German in *Die Reihe* 7 (Vienna: Universal Edition, 1960), then in English in the same issue published in London, 1965.

3. Frederic Rzewski to Wolff, letter 13 November 1964, Wolff Papers.

4. Reprinted in Christian Wolff, *Cues: Writings and Conversations* (Köln, Germany: MusikTexte, 1998) 52–54.

5. Christian George Wolff, "Aspects of the Later Plays of Euripides" (PhD dissertation, Harvard University, 1963), 1–2.

6. PEN quoted in Günter Grass and Helen Wolff, *Briefe 1959–1994*, ed. Daniela Hermes (Göttingen, Germany: Steidl, 2003), 560.

7. See John Cage and Morton Feldman, Radio Happenings (I–V, recorded at WBAI, New York City, July 1966–January 1967). At http://www.radiom.org (accessed 25 November 2011) These have also been transcribed and published as *Radio Happenings I–V: Conversations/Gespräche* (Köln, Germany: MusikTexte, 1993). For the contexts, implications, and detailed citations of all these quotations, see Michael Hicks, "'Our Webern': Cage and Feldman's Devotion to Christian Wolff," in Stephen Chase and Philip Thomas, eds., *Changing the System: The Music of Christian Wolff* (Surrey, U.K.: Ashgate, 2010), 3–5.

8. For more on this, see Michael Hicks, "Mass Marketing the American Avant Garde 1967–1971," unpublished paper delivered at the Open Space Festival of New Music, 25 March 2010, University of Northern Colorado; an earlier, shorter version was delivered at the Society for American Music Annual Meeting, 19 March 2009, Denver, Colorado.

9. Wolff to John Cage, 2 October 1967, John Cage Collection, Northwestern University Library. Hereafter cited as Cage Collection.

10. The 1960 meeting occurred when Cardew lived in Cologne, assisting Stockhausen, and Wolff took a leave from his army post to visit Cage and Cunningham, who were then visiting Cologne.

11. Frederic Rzewski to Wolff, letter 16 July 1968, Wolff Papers; Wolff to Hicks, 31 May 2008, Wolff Papers.

12. See the detailed explanation of this collection in Clemens Gresser, "*Prose Collection*: The Performer and Listener as Co-Creator," in Chase and Thomas, *Changing the System*, 193–209.

13. Cornelius Cardew, review of *Prose Collection* by Christian Wolff, *Musical Times* 110, no. 1521 (November 1969): 1171.

14. Cornelius Cardew to Wolff, letter 31 August 1969, Wolff Papers.

15. John Cage to Norman Doenges (then chairman of the Department of Classics at Dartmouth) letter 11 April 1969, Wolff Papers.

16. Wolff to Michael Hicks, email 10 June 2010. With an infant and a toddler, Wolff recalls, there were "lots of excursions to the zoo."

Chapter 4. Let Playing Be Composition and Composition Playing: 1969–1974

1. John Tilbury to Christian Wolff, letter 23 June 1969. Wolff Papers.

2. Originally published in the *Treatise Handbook* (1971), this document is now available free online at http://www.scribd.com/doc/32913735/Cornelius-Cardew-Ethic-of-Improvisation (accessed 11 February 2011).

3. Christian Wolff, *Cues: Writings and Conversations* (Köln, Germany: MusikTexte, 1998), 86.

4. The album was *An Anthology of African Music*, vol. 3, *Ba-Benzélé Pygmies* (Bärenreiter-Musicaphon BM 30 L 2303, 1965).

5. Cornelius Cardew to Wolff, letter 9 September 1971, Wolff Papers.

6. Cornelius Cardew, *Stockhausen Serves Imperialism and Other Articles* (London: Latimer New Dimensions), 40.

7. The quotations are from a page that bears the heading "From notes made in the Summer of 1972, occasioned by Cornelius Cardew's Marxist-Maoist criticism of John Cage's music (now reprinted in C.C.'s book *Stockhausen Serves Imperialism*) and by conversation with Holly Wolff." Wolff Papers.

8. Among the many sources that treat this division, see especially Wolff, "Moral Issues and Musical Practices" (1992), *Cues*, 392–94.

9. On this whole area of Wolff's career, see David Ryan, "Changing the System: Indeterminacy and Politics in the Early 1970s," and Stephen Chase, "'There Is Always a Time': Words, Music, Politics and Voice," both in Stephen Chase and Philip Thomas, eds., *Changing the System: The Music of Christian Wolff* (Surrey, U.K.: Ashgate, 2010), 143–69 and 170–89, respectively.

10. Wolff to Cornelius Cardew, letter 21 July 1972 (with annotations by Cardew), Wolff Papers.

11. The authoritative source here is Amy C. Beal, "Christian Wolff in Darmstadt, 1972 and 1974," in Chase and Thomas, *Changing the System*, 23–47.

12. For one account of fellow composers' irritation and Feldman's outburst see John Tilbury, *Cornelius Cardew (1936–1981): A Life Unfinished* (Essex, U.K.: Copula, 2008), 605.

13. Reprinted in Wolff, "What Are We Doing?" *Cues*, 98.

14. Performances notes to *Accompaniments*, in Wolff, *Cues*, 498.

15. Pantheon's 1970 edition of Jan Myrdal and Gun Kessle's *China: The Revolution Continued* was the first U.S. edition, translated from Swedish by Paul Britten Austin.

16. Donal Henahan, "Four Contemporary Piano Pieces Add New Tone to the Whitney," *New York Times*, 25 March 1970, 37.

17. Brian Dennis, "Music in London: Drumming, cpe," *Musical Times* 113, no. 1550 (April 1972): 382.

18. John Cage quoted in Frederic Rzewski, "The Algebra of Everyday Life," the preface to Wolff, *Cues*, 10.

19. This and the preceding quotation are from Wolff, "let the listeners be just as free as the players," *Cues*, 80.

20. See Richard Dufallo, *Trackings: Composers Speak with Richard Dufallo* (New York: Oxford University Press, 1989), 231–32. This episode is also discussed by Cage and Wolff

in William Duckworth, *Talking Music: Conversations with John Cage, Philip Glass, Laurie Anderson, and Five Generations of American Experimental Composers* (New York: Schirmer Books, 1995), 16 and 187.

21. Wolff talks about this in David Patterson, "Cage and Beyond: An Annotated Interview with Christian Wolff," *Perspectives of New Music* 32 (1994): 72.

22. Dufallo, *Trackings*, 121–22.

23. *For the Birds: John Cage in Conversation with Daniel Charles* (Boston: Marion Boyars, 1981; originally published in French, 1976), 136. The concert is reviewed in Henahan, "Four Contemporary Piano Pieces Add New Tone."

24. Wolff, interview by Michael Hicks, 9 March 2006. Krenek was widely held to be a second-tier twelve-tone composer.

25. Feldman in Morton Feldman, *Give My Regards to Eighth Street: Collected Writings of Morton Feldman*, ed. B. H. Friedman (Cambridge, Mass.: Exact Change, 2000), 118–19.

26. In "Morton Feldman Slee Lecture, April 15, 1973," http://ublib.buffalo.edu/libraries/units/music/spcoll/feldman/mfslee326.html (accessed 30 November 2011).

Chapter 5. Something More Specifically "Musical": 1973–1984

1. Wolff gave versions of this address at least three more times at other schools during the 1970s. While full reading copies have been lost, we rely on the set of notes he sent to Cage in 1974 (full citation below) as well as Wolff's detailed recollections of the speech.

2. From the conclusion of Cardew, "A Report on the Concert" (20 May 1973), reprinted in Chapter 3 of his *Stockhausen Serves Imperialism*.

3. John Tilbury, "Christian Wolff and the Politics of Music," notes to Christian Wolff: *Long Piano (Peace March 11)*, NewWorld Records 80699 and available online at http://www.newworldrecords.org/uploads/file9CQrs.pdf (accessed 11 February 2011).

4. John Cage to Wolff, letter 17 January 1974, Wolff Papers.

5. Wolff to John Cage, letter 15 March [1974], Wolff Papers.

6. According to David Bernstein, "Some of Wolff's transformations of source melodies bring to mind techniques used by Cage in *Cheap Imitation* (1969), *Apartment House 1776* (1976), *Quartets I–VIII* (1976), some of the *Harmony of the Maine* (1978), and *Hymns and Variations* (1979)" (email to authors, 1 July 2011).

7. John A. Lomax and Alan Lomax, *Folk Song U.S.A.* (New York: Duell, Sloan and Pearce, 1947).

8. Christian Wolff, "Music—Experiment—Education," *Sonus* 26 (Fall 2005): 29. Cage, though, it should be added, also disliked the trombone solo that Garrett List played (Exercise 17), which Cage thought too overtly expressive.

9. Wolff to John Cage, letter 17 December 1975, Cage Collection.

10. Quoted in Damon Krukowski, "Christian Wolff," *Bomb* 59 (Spring 1997), available online as http://bombsite.com/issues/59/articles/2060 (accessed 19 December 2011). See also the detailed description Wolff gives of *Wobbly Music* in an article prepared for *Sonus* (1980), reprinted in Christian Wolff, *Cues: Writings and Conversations* (Köln, Germany: MusikTexte, 1998), 138–46.

11. Frederic Rzewski to Fred Berthold, Jr., letter 9 April 1978, Wolff Papers.

12. Wolff to John Cage, letter 22 January 1980, Wolff Papers.

13. Wolff to Heinz-Klaus Metzger, letter 7 February 1978, printed in Wolff, *Cues*, 352.

14. Wolff, interview by Michael Hicks, 24 April 2007.

15. Wolff to Michael Hicks, email, 11 May 2006.

16. See John Cage and Geoffrey Barnard, *Conversation without Feldman* (Darlinghurst: Black Ram Books, 1980), 9.

17. Frederic Rzewski to Wolff, letter 24 February 1979, Wolff Papers.

18. Wolff to John Cage, letter n.d. [October 1977], Wolff Papers.

19. John Cage to Wolff, letter 3 November 1977, Wolff Papers.

Chapter 6. Not to Do Something I've Already Done: 1982–1999

1. Christian Wolff, "Under the Influence," in *Cues: Writings and Conversations* (Köln, Germany: MusikTexte, 1998), 52.

2. Cage quoted in Rzewski, "The Algebra of Everyday Life," preface to Wolff, *Cues*, 10.

3. Jon Appleton quoted in Erik Tanouye, "Quirky Music Wins Prof. $50,000 Award," *Dartmouth*, 13 January 1997.

4. Rzewski, "Algebra of Everyday Life," 10.

5. For an overview of this period, see Christopher Fox, "Exercising the Ensemble: Some Thoughts on the Later Music of Christian Wolff," in Stephen Chase and Philip Thomas, eds., *Changing the System: The Music of Christian Wolff* (Surrey, U.K.: Ashgate, 2010), 125–39.

6. Wolff, interview by Michael Hicks, 24 April 2007.

7. Ibid. In this same source, Wolff estimates that 80 percent of each piece ends up with segments in the order he wrote them, with the other 20 percent reordered or newly written.

8. Wolff to Frederic Rzewski, letter 21 July 1999, Wolff Papers.

9. Larry Polansky, interview by Christian Asplund, 20 May 2008.

10. Wolff, interview by Hicks.

11. Frederic Rzewski to Wolff, letter 16 September 1979, Wolff Papers.

12. Performance note to Wolff, Exercise 19 (Harmonic Tremors), Edition Peters, 66948 (1983).

13. *American Record Guide* review quoted in Jack Vaitayanonta, "Wolff Symposium Begins Today," *Dartmouth*, 8 January 1996.

14. The most thorough source on Wolff's orchestral music thus far is James Saunders, "Mutual Effects: Organization and Interaction in the Orchestral Music of Christian Wolff," in Chase and Thomas, *Changing the System*, 93–124.

15. Stuart Saunders Smith and Thomas De Lio, eds., *Words and Space: Anthology of Twentieth Century Musical Experiments* (New York: Rowman and Littlefield, 1989).

16. Cole Gagne, *Soundpieces 2: Interviews with American Composers* (Metuchen, N.J.: Scarecrow Press, 1993), and William Duckworth, *Talking Music: Conversations with John Cage, Philip Glass, Laurie Anderson, and Five Generations of American Experimental Composers* (New York: Schirmer Books, 1995).

17. Bunita Marcus to Michael Hicks, email, 9 December 2005; Orlando Jacinto Garcia to Michael Hicks, email, 13 December 2005.

18. In Feldman's *Three Voices* (1982), for example, Feldman uses only the half-step related pitches C♯4/D4/E♭4/E4 for the entire first page (and two later long passages). The first

two and a half minutes of *Three Voices* consist only of these four pitches. A year later, Feldman's Second String Quartet (1983) opens with these same pitches (C♯/D/E♭/E)—back in the duo's original octave—played ostinato for the first two and a half minutes. And in his solo piano work *For Bunita Marcus* (1985), Feldman uses only C♯, D, and E♭, deployed in various octaves, for the first seventy-two measures (again, about two and a half minutes).

19. "Christian Wolff: Interview by Jason Gross (April 1988)," www.furious.com/perfect/christianwolff.html (accessed 21 February 2006). Perhaps a final nod to Wolff's violin duo came in Feldman's last piano work, *Palais de Mari* (1986). There, in mm. 7–13, Feldman oscillates among the pitches D/D♯/E—all in the duo's original soprano octave. As though it were an isolated but obligatory citation of Wolff, nothing like it occurs in the nearly twenty-five minutes of music that follow.

20. Wolff took inspiration from György Kurtág for what he called these "individual declarations of friendship" in music. Wolff to Michael Hicks, email 11 May 2006.

21. Wolff in James Saunders, ed., *The Ashgate Research Companion to Experimental Music* (Surrey, U.K.: Ashgate, 2009), 364.

22. Wolff, interview by Hicks.

23. Ibid.

24. Wolff in Saunders, *Ashgate Research Companion*, 363.

25. "Christian Wolff and Classics," a document prepared for and sent to Hicks on 5 December 2010 by Wolff's friend and colleague James Tatum, reflecting back on that Wolff symposium.

26. Christian Wolff, "Crossings of Experimental Music and Greek Tragedy," in Peter Brown and Suzana Ograjensek, eds., *Ancient Drama in Music for the Modern Stage* (New York: Oxford, 2010), 304.

27. Wolff, 1996–97 faculty productivity report for Dartmouth, copy in authors' possession.

28. Wolff quoted in Tanouye, "Quirky Music Wins Prof. $50,000 Award."

29. Wolff in his liner notes to *Christian Wolff: Complete Music for Violin and Piano*, Mode Records 126 (2003).

30. Wolff to Frederic Rzewski, letters 16 and 21 July 1999, Wolff Papers.

31. Among the works are a few revisions or arrangements of earlier works.

Chapter 7. Among Friends, in a Private World

1. For the quotations and general discussion, see Christian Wolff, "Aspects of the Later Plays of Euripides" (PhD dissertation, Harvard University, 1963), 158, 161–64.

2. Vivien Schweitzer, "Composers of a Certain Age Receive a Makeover," *New York Times*, 24 May 2008.

3. From his "Sketch of a Statement," written in April 1993, distributed privately then published in the program booklet *Christian Wolff: The Composer and the Classicist Symposium and Music Festival Dartmouth College, January 8–10, 1996*, Wolff Papers.

4. See Harold C. Schonberg, "New Music, Some Cute, Some Serious," *New York Times*, 12 April 1974.

5. See Liz Ellison, "Music Prof Gains Recognition with Experimental 'Exercises,'" *Dartmouth*, 31 January 2007.

6. Steven Johnson, ed., *The New York Schools of Music and the Visual Arts* (New York: Routledge, 2001).

7. Tamsen Wolff to Michael Hicks, email 7 June 2006.

8. Tristram Wolff to Michael Hicks, email 9 May 2006.

9. "Transcript of Christian Wolff Seminar," Ostrava Days, 2001, at http://www.ocnmh.cz/days2001_transkript_wolff.htm (accessed 13 February 2011).

10. Wolff discusses this piece, along with other recent works, in Stephen Chase and Clemens Gresser, "Ordinary Matters: Christian Wolff on His Recent Music," *Tempo* 58, no. 229 (2004): 19–27.

11. Wolff, interview by Michael Hicks, 24 April 2007.

12. From the work's program note, available at http://www.ocnmh.cz/biographies_wolff.htm (accessed 20 December 2011).

13. Wolff to Michael Hicks, letter 18 February 2011.

14. Wolff in James Saunders, ed., *The Ashgate Research Companion to Experimental Music* (Surrey, U.K.: Ashgate, 2009), 363.

15. See the square and a discussion of it in Stephen Chase and Philip Thomas, eds., *Changing the System: The Music of Christian Wolff* (Surrey, U.K.: Ashgate, 2010), 79–81.

16. Frederic Rzewski to Wolff, email 31 March 2007, Wolff Papers.

17. Wolff, interview by Hicks.

18. Ibid.

19. Wolff to Michael Hicks, letter 18 February 2011.

20. Ibid.

21. See Carl Dahlhaus, "New Music as Historical Category," in *Schoenberg and the New Music* (Cambridge: University of Cambridge, 1987), 1–13.

22. Wolff to Hicks, 18 February 2011.

23. Wolff, interview by Michael Hicks, 26 March 2010.

24. See Christopher Thomas Miller, *Games: Purpose and Potential in Education* (New York: Springer Science and Business Media, 2008), 19.

25. "Improvisation, Heterophony, Politics, Composition: Panel Discussion with Christian Wolff, Larry Polansky, Kui Dong, Christian Asplund, and Michael Hicks," *Perspectives of New Music* 45 (Summer 2007): 138.

26. Willie Winant, interview by Christian Asplund, 20 May 2008.

27. "Improvisation, Heterophony, Politics, Composition," 138.

28. From a lecture-discussion by Wolff at the University of Northern Colorado (Greeley), 25 March 2010 (notes taken by Michael Hicks at the event).

29. Wolff in Saunders, *Ashgate Research Companion*, 361.

30. Larry Polansky, interview by Christian Asplund, 20 May 2008.

31. Wolff, "Aspects of the Later Plays of Euripides," 164.

FOR FURTHER READING

A reader most often encounters references to Christian Wolff in works about John Cage. The catalog of such works is relatively vast, too much so to recapitulate here. We've noted below a few items either more particular to Wolff or more general about his colleagues and their techniques. *Cues* (see in the By Wolff section) anthologizes all of the best published material by Wolff through 1998. *Changing the System* (see in the About Wolff section) contains important articles by nine scholars as well as the most complete (and annotated) Wolff worklist through the early 2000s.

By Wolff

Cues: Writings and Conversations. 1998. Köln, Germany: MusikTexte.

"Music—Experiment—Education." 2005. *Sonus* 26, no. 1 (Fall): 18–36.

"Experimental Music around 1950 and Some Consequences and Causes (Social-Political and Musical)." 2009. *American Music* 27 (Winter): 424–40.

"Crossings of Experimental Music and Greek Tragedy." 2010. In Peter Brown and Suzana Ograjensek, eds., *Ancient Drama in Music for the Modern Stage.* New York: Oxford.

Interviews with Wolff

Duckworth, William. 1995. *Talking Music: Conversations with John Cage, Philip Glass, Laurie Anderson, and Five Generations of American Experimental Composers.* New York: Schirmer Books.

A Chance Encounter with Christian Wolff: Friday, January 11, 2002, 4:33 PM at the Greenwich House Music School (New York, NY). 2002. Interview with Frank J. Oteri, 11 January, www.newmusicbox.org/35/interview_wolff.pdf (accessed 20 December 2011).

"Christian Wolff Seminar (an excerpt)." 2003. From *Ostrava Days 2003 Report* at www.ocnmh.cz/days2003_lectures_wolff.htm (accessed 20 December 2011).

About Wolff

Chase, Stephen, and Philip Thomas, eds. 2010. *Changing the System: The Music of Christian Wolff.* Surrey, U.K.: Ashgate.

On the New York School

Johnson, Steven, ed. 2001. *The New York Schools of Music and the Visual Arts.* New York: Routledge.

Gresser, Clemens. 2004. "(Re-)Defining the Relationships between Composer, Performer and Listener: Earle Brown, John Cage, Morton Feldman and Christian Wolff." PhD dissertation, University of Southampton.

Brown, Carolyn. 2007. *Chance and Circumstance: Twenty Years with Cage and Cunningham.* New York: Knopf.

On Indeterminacy and Experimental Music

Behrman, David. 1965. "What Indeterminate Notation Determines." *Perspectives of New Music* 3, no. 2 (Spring–Summer): 58–73.

Smalley, Roger. 1969–70. "Some Aspects of the Changing Relationship between Composer and Performer in Contemporary Music." *Proceedings of the Royal Music Association* 96:73–84.

Holzaepfel, John. 1994. "David Tudor and the Performance of American Experimental Music 1950–1959." PhD dissertation, City University of New York.

"Improvisation, Heterophony, Politics, Composition: Panel Discussion with Christian Wolff, Larry Polansky, Kui Dong, Christian Asplund, and Michael Hicks." 2007. *Perspectives of New Music* 45 (Summer): 133–49.

Kim, Rebecca Y. 2008. "In No Uncertain Musical Terms: The Cultural Politics of John Cage's Indeterminacy." PhD dissertation, Columbia University.

Tilbury, John. 2008. *Cornelius Cardew (1936–1981): A Life Unfinished.* Essex, U.K.: Copula.

Saunders, James, ed. 2009. *The Ashgate Research Companion to Experimental Music.* Surrey, U.K.: Ashgate.

RECORDINGS

While a fine Wolff discography appears in *Changing the System*—and we defer to it as a master list—it is in some ways obsolete. That is not just because Wolff discs have continued to appear but because discographies as such mean less and less in an era of blogs, file sharing, bootleg recordings, YouTube, and other means of transmission that, as we write this, can only be imagined.

Throughout the book we refer to many of Wolff's recordings. In the 1960s there were two LPs, one on a new independent label (Mainstream, 1963) and the other on Columbia's budget label (Odyssey, 1968). The latter of these included the piece *For 1, 2 or 3 People* played by David Tudor. What is best about that recording is that it would be the first of several for a piece that thrives mainly on its reimagining. No one recording could convey the piece's essence; each new recording utterly redefines the work's sound and shape. In the 1970s four new Wolff recordings appeared, two of them on fairly stable European labels (Wergo, Odeon). In the 1980s, four more appeared (including another of *For 1, 2 or 3*).

It was not until the 1990s that the ease of producing and manufacturing compact discs (which contain more clock time and dynamic range than LPs) enabled many more Wolff recordings to emerge. The Hat Hut label alone gave us six Wolff CDs in that decade, including an archival disc of Tudor and Cage playing two versions of Wolff's Duo for Pianists 1 in 1960. In the 2000s the Mode and Matchless labels gave us seven CDs between them. Add these to an array of independent pressings on smaller labels, and we now have multiple recordings of fundamental Wolff works, including *For 1, 2 and 3*, *Edges*, and the exercises.

A few archival CDs of various Wolff performances (including orchestral works) circulate in the music-collecting underground. On the Art of the States website (http://artofthestates.org/cgi-bin/piece.pl?pid=214) one may hear Wolff's Trio III (1996). The Dartmouth website http://digitalmusics.dartmouth.edu/~larry/trio/trio.index.html features recordings of trio improvisations (1999–2009) by Wolff,

Kui Dong, and Larry Polansky. YouTube harbors dozens of recordings of Wolff pieces (some involving Wolff himself as performer). At least one film (*Who Gets to Call It Art?*, a 2006 documentary about Henry Geldzahler) includes Wolff's 1950 Serenade in its soundtrack—a fact that even Wolff didn't know until we told him.

These latter entries are little more than suggestive of what one encounters in the postcorporate recording world. Wolff himself feels little territoriality about realizations of his work, although some he prefers to others. The player-friendly nature of many of his scores suggests an access-friendly promulgation of their sound.

INDEX

MICHAEL HICKS is a professor of music at Brigham Young University and the author of *Sixties Rock: Garage, Psychedelic, and Other Satisfactions* and other works.

CHRISTIAN ASPLUND is an associate professor of music and composer-in-residence at Brigham Young University.

AMERICAN

Composers

Lou Harrison
Leta E. Miller and Fredric Lieberman

John Cage
David Nicholls

Dudley Buck
N. Lee Orr

William Grant Still
Catherine Parsons Smith

Rudolf Friml
William Everett

Elliott Carter
James Wierzbicki

Carla Bley
Amy C. Beal

Christian Wolff
Michael Hicks and Christian Asplund

The University of Illinois Press
is a founding member of the
Association of American University Presses.

Composed in 9.5/13 Janson Text LT Std
with Meta display
by Barbara Evans
at the University of Illinois Press
Manufactured by Sheridan Books, Inc.

University of Illinois Press
1325 South Oak Street
Champaign, IL 61820-6903
www.press.uillinois.edu